Newfields

Newfields

a place
for nature
& the arts

Generous support for this publication was provided by Kay Koch as well as The National Bank of Indianapolis

page 2 Robert Irwin (American, b. 1928), *Light and Space III*, 2008, fluorescent lights, approximately 40 × 25 ft. (installed). Purchased with funds provided by Ann M. and Chris Stack, The Ballard Fund, Nancy Foxwell Neuberger Acquisition Endowment Fund, Anonymous IV Art Fund, Lucille Stewart Endowed Art Fund, Martha M. Shertzer Art Purchase Fund in Memory of Her Nephew, Charles S. Sands, Roger G. Wolcott Fund, Gift of the Alliance of the Indianapolis Museum of Art, Frank Curtis Springer & Irving Moxley Springer Purchase Fund, E. Hardey Adriance Fine Arts Acquisition Fund in memory of Marguerite Hardey Adriance, Emma Harter Sweetser Fund, Mr. and Mrs. Richard Crane Fund, Elizabeth S. Lawton Fine Art Fund, Cecil F. Head Art Fund, Mary V. Black Art Endowment Fund, General Endowed Art Fund, Mr. and Mrs. Theodore P. Van Vorhees Art Fund, General Memorial Art Fund, General Art Fund.

page 3 Fernand Léger (French, 1881–1955), *Man and Woman* (detail), 1921, oil on canvas, 36¼ × 25½ in. Martha Delzell Memorial Fund, 52.28.

facing page Robert Indiana (American, b. 1928), *LOVE*, 1970, Cor-ten steel, 144 × 144 × 72 in. Gift of the Friends of the Indianapolis Museum of Art in memory of Henry F. DeBoest. Restoration was made possible by Patricia J. and James E. LaCrosse, 75.174. Sol LeWitt (American, 1928–2007), *Wall Drawing No. 652, Continuous Forms With Color Acrylic Washes Superimposed* (detail), 1990, acrylic wash on wall, 30 × 60 ft. Gift of the Dudley Sutphin Family, 1990.40. Fernand Léger (French, 1881–1955), *Man and Woman* (detail), 1921, oil on canvas, 36¼ × 25½ in. Martha Delzell Memorial Fund, 52.28.

foreword

IT WAS IN THE LATE 1960S THAT THE OLDFIELDS ESTATE WAS given by the Lilly family to the Art Association of Indianapolis to be its new home. In 1969, with a museum building under construction at the site, the Art Association adopted a new name: The Indianapolis Museum or Art. Much has changed in the nearly 50 years since ground was broken on that new building. Collections have grown, galleries have expanded, gardens have multiplied, and an expansive park and historic properties have been added. As 2017 draws to a close, the institution once again finds itself at a crossroads. Thanks to a generous grant from the Lilly Endowment, several major studies have recently been completed that analyzed our art collections, community engagement, brand, business operations, philanthropic fundraising, and potential growth in visitation, membership, and earned income. This highly informative research laid the foundation for a new master plan now underway. This effort is led by the well-known landscape architecture and urban design studio, David Rubin LAND COLLECTIVE from Philadelphia. The result of the firm's work will be a 30-year road map for the future—one that addresses access, infrastructure, connectivity, and space needs with an eye to improve both our visitors' experiences with art and nature and to increase both donated and earned income.

As its physical and financial landscape has changed, the cultural landscape in which the Indianapolis Museum of Art exists has also shifted dramatically. Armed with a new and deeper understanding of how visitors now want to engage with art and nature, and how our brand was perceived by the majority of Indianapolis' residents, the organization recently decided to give our entire 152-acre campus a name for the first time. **Newfields** was chosen because it evokes the spirit of new fields of thinking, and creates a historic connection to the site as "new" property that Mr. and Mrs. J.K. Lilly Jr. acquired to enlarge their Oldfields estate. That said, the name for our great museum is not going away. Rather, the Indianapolis Museum of Art name will be used specifically for the art museum building and its associate public programs. We feel that, by naming the entire campus, a larger potential audience will understand more clearly the rich array of experiences with art AND nature available on this magnificent campus.

That brings us to this present work. While the institution has published widely, including many volumes about its art collections, history, and historic properties, there has never been a volume written for the general public that provides an overview of all this institution has to offer both indoors and out. The book that you hold in your hands is an attempt to rectify that and to present the dynamic diversity of Newfields in a visually engaging format. It draws upon those earlier works and adds to them while also providing a glimpse of where this great institution will be heading in its next century and a third.

Charles L. Venable, PhD
Melvin & Bren Simon Director and CEO

acknowledgments

A WORK LIKE THIS IS NOT POSSIBLE WITHOUT THE SUPPORT and assistance of a number of individuals. I would first like to thank the authors of *Every Way Possible: 125 Years of the Indianapolis Museum of Art, The Story of the IMA, Miller House and Garden,* and *Oldfields:* Anne P. Robinson, S.L. Berry, David S. Powell, Julianna Thibodeaux, Jane Graham, and Bradley C. Brooks, excerpts of whose works have been adapted for this present volume. Thanks are also due to The National Bank of Indianapolis and Kay Koch, both of whom provided generous support for its production.

For guidance and review of the text, I offer my heartfelt appreciation to former Wood-Pulliam Distinguished Senior Curator Ellen W. Lee, former Curator of Prints and Drawings Marty Krause, Curator of Asian Art John Teramoto, Curator of Special Projects Annette Schlagenhauff, Curator of Textile and Fashion Arts Niloo Paydar, and former Curator of Contemporary Art Tricia Paik. For review and for sharing their knowledge of the gardens and historic properties, I extend my thanks to former Ruth Lilly Deputy Director of Horticulture Mark Zelonis, as well as current Director of Horticulture Chad Franer. I would also like to acknowledge Deputy Director of Marketing and External Affairs Gary Stoppelman and former Director of Marketing Susie McKenna for their work on the institution's rebranding efforts, and to thank Director of Retail Services Jenny Geiger for her support of this project.

For capturing the beauty of Newfields and helping present it in all of its diversity, I'm indebted to Assistant Director of Photography Tascha Horowitz, as well as Senior Photographer Eric Lubrick. Image permissions were deftly handled by Manager of Rights and Reproductions Anne Young, and Editor and Manager of Publications Dylan R. Jensen patiently shepherded the manuscript through the production process.

Lastly, although no words can adequately convey my thanks, I would like to express my profound sense of appreciation to the donors, volunteers, patrons, guests, and staff members who have been instrumental to the success of the institution over the years.

—C.V.

newfields overview

EXTRAORDINARY ART, MAJESTIC TREES, BLOOMING ORCHIDS, and a tranquil lake are just a few of the wonders that make Newfields a magical place where art and nature come together unlike anywhere else. Here guests can explore a major art museum, a 100-acre park, a 52-acre garden, and a 1913 mansion house all on a single campus, as well as satellite properties featuring a 1920s estate and a Modernist house and garden from the 1950s. Newfields truly has something for everyone.

Newfields is the creation of generations of passionate volunteers, staff, donors, and an engaged public. While key individuals stand out along its arc of history, Newfields is not the work of a single great art collector or wealthy family, but rather an institution that has grown alongside the city of Indianapolis thanks to the contributions of countless supporters over many decades. With more than 50,000 works of art, 170 acres of land, and 18 buildings, Newfields is among the largest museum and garden complexes in the United States.

The experience of art and nature is at the heart of Newfields. Millions of visitors have enhanced their lives at Newfields, and no doubt millions more will as the institution advances the use of innovative technology, experimental programming, and community outreach to attract and engage new and broader audiences. Whether they are four-year-olds learning in its onsite preschool, college students doing assignments in the galleries, or senior citizens recharging in the gardens, people from all walks of life have enjoyed and learned from this living place where great art and wondrous nature meet in exceptional ways.

Newfields embodies a few key principles. First is **Preservation**. On its campus are thousands of irreplaceable works of art and historical objects. Among its most precious artifacts are two

page 8 Paul Gauguin (French, 1848–1903), *Still Life with Profile of Laval* (detail), 1886, oil on canvas, 18⅛ × 15 in. Samuel Josefowitz Collection of the School of Pont-Aven, through the generosity of Lilly Endowment Inc., the Josefowitz Family, Mr. and Mrs. James M. Cornelius, Mr. and Mrs. Leonard J. Betley, Lori and Dan Efroymson, and other Friends of the Museum, 1998.167.

page 9 Guests view works by the Old Masters in the Clowes Pavilion, 2015. Artwork: Rembrandt van Rijn (Dutch, 1606–1669), *Self-Portrait,* about 1629, oil on panel, 17½ × 13½ × ¾ in. (panel) 27½ × 24 × 3 in. (framed). Courtesy of The Clowes Fund, C10063.

below Summer campers work on an activity by the Rain Garden, 2015.

facing page Artist Julianne Swartz installing her exhibition *Julianne Swartz: How Deep Is Your,* March 14–June 15, 2014, in the June M. McCormack Forefront Galleries.

homes with gardens that are both designated National Historic Landmarks and another whose neighborhood is on the National Historic Register. Living treasures, too, count among Newfields' greatest assets, as do its waterways, which include fountains, a lake, a canal, and a river. In addition there are libraries and archives holding large numbers of books, photographs, manuscripts, and sound recordings. Today Newfields works endlessly to safeguard all the treasures in its care, presenting them to its current visitors while preserving them for future generations.

Next is **Education and Training**. When founded over 130 years ago, the institution was both a museum and an art school that educated the public about art and trained artists. Although the museum and school separated in 1967, both the Indianapolis Museum of Art at Newfields and the John Herron School of Art

continue their educational missions, as does Newfields as a whole. Educators, curators, horticulturalists, scientists, conservators, and trained docents engage the public each day. Annually, thousands of students flow into the galleries and out into the gardens, park, and historic homes. The youngest participate in Newfields' preschool, while college students do research and serve as interns. A host of workshops, demonstrations, talks, films, and performances attract lifelong learners of all ages.

With a major art museum, **Art Historical and Conservation Research** are of great importance. Through the years, scores of curators and conservators have worked to better understand the museum's art collection and its historic properties and to share their discoveries. Today curators oversee a diverse array of art from around the world that spans 5,000 years of human creativity. Simultaneously, conservators work in their laboratories investigating and preserving the art collection. At present, it is one of the few museums that maintain labs for conserving works on paper, paintings, objects, and textiles, as well as a laboratory for pure science as it relates to art. Through the effort of its curatorial, conservation, and science staff, the museum has enlarged and refined its collections and produced a distinguished record of publications on myriad subjects. In addition, libraries and archives provide a rich resource for researchers, while its online databases bring the art collection, library, archives, and programming to individuals around the globe.

Because Newfields is also a great garden and park, it is truly a "living museum." Thus, **Horticulture and Natural Resource Management** are key. This commitment began in the late 1960s when the Indianapolis Museum of Art moved to the Oldfields estate, the former home of Mr. and Mrs. J.K. Lilly Jr. and their family. Professional horticulturalists, natural resource managers, and preservationists work tirelessly to maintain the essence of both the historic gardens and the wider ecosystem in the form of the Virginia B. Fairbanks Art & Nature Park, a 100-acre urban oasis. Through their efforts, university students advance their studies in horticulture and land management, children experience the wonders and healing power of nature and history, and volunteers contribute meaningfully to enhance the public's experience with the great outdoors. However, Newfields' commitment to nature goes beyond human beings to include a wide array of animals and countless numbers of plants. In all, Newfields horticulturalists

and land managers care for more than 800 genera of plants, 2,000 hybrids and species, and over 600,000 square feet of turf. Just minutes from downtown Indianapolis, Newfields has become a unique oasis in the heart of a bustling city, where one can learn about art and nature or simply refresh in a hectic world.

Everything Newfields does is for the public, so **Public Programming and Audience Experiences** are central to the institution's mission. In fact the official mission of Newfields is "to enrich lives through exceptional experiences with art and nature." In a society where technology puts the world in the palm of one's hand, visitors want their Newfields experience to engage them sensorially, intellectually, and physically. No longer is it sufficient to hang great artworks in galleries and have guests passively stroll by them. Current audiences want to be part of the action, to explore art and nature on their own terms, and to make connections they find relevant to their own lives. To keep up with its ever-changing audience, Newfields strives to engage people through innovation and creativity. There are curators, horticulturalists, educators, evaluators, designers, and programmers who develop and manage a huge array of public programs each and every day, which are held in spaces that include galleries, a park, gardens, greenhouses, and three theaters. The breadth of programming astonishes—from art history lessons, to film series, to hummingbird banding.

Hospitality and Community Engagement are natural characteristics of Newfields, given its location in the heart of the Midwest. Since the founding of the museum over 130 years ago, the institution has welcomed guests from around the world. However, its main focus is serving the greater Indianapolis community and surrounding region. To that end, Newfields features spaces— ranging from classrooms to the elegant Randolph H. Deer and Wayne P. Zink Special Events Pavilion, where corporations, not-for-profits, charities, and families can work or celebrate. Similarly, while individuals and groups of all kinds visit Newfields daily, special initiatives take art and nature out into the community. Wide-ranging programs are designed to appeal to diverse audiences, including those who are economically challenged.

Finally, Innovation and Sustainability undergird all that Newfields does. Since the challenges of the future will be different from those of the past, new ideas must be experimented with to ensure that older public programs and business models are still effective. To continue to perform at an exceptionally high level and to remain relevant to its audiences, the institution needs to constantly innovate. In the area of finance, for example, Newfields can no longer rely on its endowment to cover the vast majority of its expenses and is thus exploring new ways to broaden its audience thereby increasing membership, earned income, and philanthropic support. Likewise, ecological sustainability is also vitally important to Newfields. Through the years it has greatly reduced the amount of energy it uses to heat and light the galleries and the level of pesticides it uses in the gardens and park. The staff has replaced invasive plant species with native ones, created a rain garden to purify parking-lot runoff, channeled rainwater down to the park to feed its wetlands, and built habitats for wildlife.

Going forward, all these efforts will grow exponentially as Newfields works to unite its multifaceted campus into a more holistic experience of art and nature. Numerous studies show that younger and more diverse audiences than those who have traditionally come to the museum want to spend more time with their friends and family outdoors. Unlike a stand-alone art museum,

Installation view of *Tradition Reborn: Contemporary Japanese Ceramics*, July 31, 2015–September 18, 2016, in the Valeria J. Medveckis Gallery.

Newfields can capitalize on this trend by investing more in its natural resources and related programming. For example, Newfields activities now embrace a seasonal programming model that more strategically unites activities in the galleries with those in the gardens and park each season. In the gardens this means a more dramatic visual program of enhanced color in spring as thousands of new bulbs burst into bloom. Summer sees amazing sweeps of color and dramatic plant displays that give way in fall to vibrant foliage, pumpkins, and festive activities that everyone can enjoy. To celebrate the close of one year and the beginning of another, Newfields developed a stronger holiday tradition that will bring more visitors back annually to see the beautiful gardens and Lilly House aglow with lights, along with festive experiences in the museum. In both the gardens and park, additional infrastructure is being put in place to allow more guests to access these wonderful amenities, while enabling Newfields to better host festivals that attract thousands of people, like the Penrod Arts Fair that has been held on the campus for over 50 years.

Over the coming decade dramatic changes will also come to the galleries. Already within the past few years visitor satisfaction with the museum's major exhibitions has increased dramatically. Guests can now dive more deeply into art than they could before thanks to innovative uses of video, sound, and texts delivered through a skillful employment of technology. Such success will be brought to the permanent collection galleries, so the public can experience the museum's greatest masterpieces in ways never before possible. Curators, conservators, and scientists are now working with educators, programmers, and technologists to co-develop exhibitions and installations that meld art history, scientific analysis, and innovative technologies in new and surprising ways. Even the traditional manner of presenting art by time, geography, and media are blurring as younger audiences want more powerful experiences that transcend these boundaries.

These first bold moves in support of the new strategic plan have already shown results. In the financial realm, for example, a thorough analysis has been made of all of Newfields' business operations with the goal of better understanding the impact of everything the institution does. A new long-term debt repayment plan is being developed and both interest and principal payments are now being made annually. With respect to the endowment, Newfields will return to an interest draw of 5% or less by 2018,

which will allow the endowment's principal to grow more consistently. At of the end of 2016 the endowment was valued at $343 million and was ranked the 15th largest among U.S. art museums.

However, the best measure of a great institution is not its significance to the economy, but its importance to the people it serves. The signs here are very positive as well. Newfields membership, for example, now stands at an all-time high, and it has more college student members than ever before.

facing page A conservator retouches an Italian Renaissance painting in the Clowes Pavilion, 2015. Artwork: Jacopo Zucchi (Italian, 1540–1596), *Portrait of a Lady* (detail), 2016.162, oil on canvas, 48 × 37¾ in. The Clowes Collection, 2016.162.

above Summer campers take part in a DJ dance party in the Caroline Marmon Fesler Gallery, 2015. Artwork: Julianne Swartz (American, b. 1967), *Terrain* (detail), 2008, 14- and 18-gauge colored electrical wire, speakers, and sound, 240 × 692 × 347 in. (installed). Martha Delzell Memorial Fund, 2010.69.

the museum

chapter two

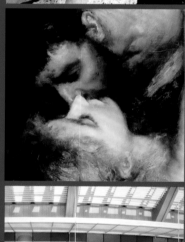

The Early Years

In 1883, the year the Indianapolis Museum of Art was founded, Indiana was still considered part of the "the West." Despite this, Indianapolis, its centrally located capital, was a bustling city of 75,000 and well connected by rail to the rest of country. It also boasted a small number of civic-minded leaders passionate about culture and the arts. May Wright Sewall (1844–1920) was such a leader. An educator and activist, Sewall was nationally prominent in the women's suffrage and world peace movements. She and her husband, the Harvard-educated Theodore Sewall, routinely hosted speakers and welcomed large groups into their home to discuss political and cultural issues. These salons routinely drew crowds of 100 to 200 people, and the success of one such gathering, a lecture on etchings and engravings by the writer Nancy Adsit, prompted May Wright Sewall to invite those present to meet again to discuss the organization of a society for the study and promotion of art in Indianapolis.

Several attempts had been made since the 1850s to found an art association in Indianapolis, but none of them had been long-lived. May Wright Sewall's efforts were more effective, and in April 1883 articles of association were drawn up and signed by Sewell and 17 other women. The purpose of the new organization was:

"To cultivate and advance Art in all its branches, to provide means for instruction in the various branches of Art; to establish for that end a permanent gallery, and also to establish and produce lectures upon subjects relevant to Art."

A public meeting was held on May 7 at which a constitution and work plan were adopted, and on October 11 the Art Association of Indianapolis was formally incorporated with 54 male and female,

16

dues-paying members. Functioning as an open-membership club, the Association held meetings in members' homes and worked to provide professional art education and opportunities for citizens to learn and engage with visual art. Its inaugural exhibition opened in November 1883 at the English Hotel on the Circle downtown and contained 453 paintings lent by galleries, collectors, and artists in New York, Chicago, and Detroit. The first purchases for the new Association's permanent collection were made from such early shows, including Percival de Luce's *An Anxious Mother* and Gustav Wertheimer's *The Kiss of the Siren.* Although it was retained in the collection, the latter soon proved controversial and was banned from public view after it was deemed "unfit" for children's eyes.

While it organized exhibitions and collected art, the Art Association also tried to move forward with starting an art school. Others had attempted to found an art academy in Indianapolis before, and the Association's initial efforts likewise floundered. Classes began in 1884 with a part-time instructor and 30 students. First located at the Denison Hotel and later at Plymouth Church, the school closed after only two years due to lack of funds. It would take the bequest of John Herron to transform the Art Association.

John Herron Art Institute

The finances of the young Art Association were entirely dependent upon membership dues and admission income from its exhibitions and events. Thus it was imperative for the organization to raise and sustain public interest in its cause. Although May Wright Sewall and the other founders often found that the general public was not as motivated by art as they were, the group persevered, believing that the Association was making an important contribution that was to provide Indianapolis with the ennobling influence of art. Sewell, in an account of these formative years, wrote, "Nothing is so cosmopolitan in its tendency as art; where it flourishes, the provincial spirit declines; sect and party lines become faint as it becomes dominant. The art spirit is by no means dominant in Indianapolis, but it is felt as a vital force."

What brought energy to that "vital force" was a $225,000 bequest from the obscure John Herron (1817–1895). Born in England, Herron immigrated with his parents to the United States where his father eventually established a successful farming operation in Mount Carmel, Indiana. In 1869, at age 52, John married Electra D. Turrell, and 12 years later the couple moved to

page 17 Indianapolis-based artist and art teacher Wilhelmina Seegmiller with schoolchildren viewing the permanent collection at the John Herron Art Institute, November 24, 1909, Historical Photography Collection (PHO002), IMA Archives.

above and page 16 Mary Wright Sewall, circa 1880, taken by the Indianapolis photography studio Marceau & Power. Library of Congress Prints and Photographs Division, LC-USZ62-75447.

facing page and page 16 Gustav Wertheimer (German, 1847–1902), *The Kiss of the Siren*, 1882, oil on canvas, 85 × 112 in. Anonymous Gift. The painting was accessioned twice, first as 86.1 in 1886 and then as 76.27 in 1976.

Indianapolis. Few civic leaders would have known Herron when he lived in the city between 1881 and 1894, and he was never a member of the Art Association. But he invested in real estate, made money, and never took on debt. The Herrons did not have children, and Electra died in 1892. Soon John Herron's health began to decline and he traveled west for medical treatment. Weak and partially blind, John Herron died in Los Angeles on April 30, 1895.

While he lived a rather quiet life, John Herron's death created a sensation. The exact motivation of his bequest was, and remains, something of a mystery. However, in a speech commemorating him in 1905, one Association member ventured that "Mr. Herron seems to have been impressed with the fact that it was necessary for humanity to get away from the absorbing business of life, to yield for a little while to the influences of art and nature." In today's dollars the Herron bequest to the fledging Art Association would be worth more than $6 million. Instantly the Association was a wealthy institution, and on May 25, 1895, over 400 people attended a meeting at Indianapolis's Grand Opera House to celebrate the

above left John Herron (1817–1895), first major benefactor of the Art Association of Indianapolis, Historical Photography Collection (PHO002), IMA Archives.

above right Herron School of Art building, June 6, 1923, Historical Photography Collection (PHO002), IMA Archives.

facing page Public school children waiting in line in the Sculpture Court of the John Herron Art Institute to take a guided tour, February 5, 1915, Historical Photography Collection (PHO002), IMA Archives.

miracle. Herron's only stipulation was to build a gallery and art school in his name. Although this request neatly coincided with the Art Association's goals, exactly how to spend its newfound wealth became a complicated issue fraught with divergent opinions. In the end the Herron bequest was divided into three funds: $150,000 for art acquisitions, $10,000 for operating the art school, and $65,000 for a new school and gallery. Ten years passed, however, between the time the bequest was made and ground was broken for the new building. In late 1906 the newly christened John Herron Art Institute held a grand opening for its new home at 16th and Pennsylvania Streets. The restrained Beaux-Arts style building had been designed by the local firm of Vonnegut & Bohn, which also

designed an additional structure that opened in 1908 to house the art school. Over the next six decades the Herron Art Institute matured and expanded on this site just north of downtown. Under the leadership of a series of museum and art school directors, the Institute became increasingly professional and its art collection more international and of higher quality. Scores of artists were trained at Herron, while thousands of schoolchildren streamed through the galleries annually. Museum programming was extremely varied, ranging from plays to lectures, concerts, and the development of a library. Special emphasis was placed on educating schoolchildren who often accounted for fully half of the attendance.

In 1929 a much larger building for the John Herron Art Institute opened. In keeping with the increasingly cosmopolitan nature of the institution, the architect for this new structure was French-born Paul Philippe Cret, whose other notable commissions included the Indianapolis Central Library, the Detroit Institute of Arts, and the Rodin Museum in Philadelphia. The new facility greatly improved art instruction, but the financial health of the organization suffered as the country slid into economic depression. World War II and the economic boom that followed brought new vigor to the Institute under the leadership of board president Caroline Marmon Fesler. Not only did she acquire a series of exceptional works of art by Modernists like Cézanne, Picasso, and Van Gogh, Fesler personally made large donations to renovate and expand the galleries. Upon her death in 1960, she bequeathed her art collection and left $500,000 for the construction of new buildings on the 16th Street campus.

Despite the dedication in 1962 of Fesler Hall, some supporters were calling for the Herron Institute of Art to leave its original site. The postwar financial recovery had led to steady growth on Indianapolis' north side, and some argued that the Institute should move north to be closer to its primary supporters. Others felt it should move downtown to be central to the entire city and become part of plans to redevelop Indianapolis's core. The deciding event occurred in 1966 when siblings J.K. Lilly III and Ruth Lilly donated their parents' estate to the Institute. Called Oldfields, the verdant, 52-acre property located at 38th Street and Michigan Road was further north and provided ample room for future growth within a lush, garden setting. However, the art school did not make the move. Worried about accreditation issues and the ability to support both a museum and art school, the board voted in July 1967 to transfer the art school to Indiana University. With new oversight, the John Herron School of Art continued to grow and is now considered one of the country's best. In 2004 it moved from its 16th Street location to a new facility downtown on the campus of IUPUI (Indiana University–Purdue University Indianapolis). The original buildings of the John Herron Art Institute became the home of Herron High School, a public charter school offering a classical liberal arts education.

left Caroline Marmon Fesler at the commencement ceremony of the Herron Art School, June 11, 1940. Caroline Marmon Fesler succeeded Evans Woollen as president of the Art Association in 1942. *The Indianapolis News*, June 12, 1940, Publicity Scrapbooks, IMA Archives.

facing page The Herman C. and Ellnora D. Krannert Pavilion entrance lit up at night soon after opening, 1970. Gift of Ambrose M. Richardson and William C. Wright, Historical Photography Archives (PHO002), IMA Archives.

A New Home: 1970 Building

With the issue of the Museum's location settled, the board turned its attention to building a new facility. Ambrose Madison Richardson, based in Champaign-Urbana, Illinois, was selected as architect and asked to design the new building and a plan for its future growth. Richardson's "less is more" approach was heavily influenced by the German-born Modernist architects Mies van der Rohe and Walter Gropius. As a result, both the overall plan and the original main building were designed as simple geometric masses with restrained, classically proportioned detailing.

A strong force behind the museum's new building was Herman Krannert, a successful businessman and art collector who served as chairman of the Art Association's board from 1960 to 1972. He had previously worked with Ambrose Richardson and was highly involved in the development of the architectural project. In fact, Krannert was so engaged by the work that he and his wife, Ellnora, gave the lead gift of $3 million to the construction project. At a ceremony attended by thousands of people, the Krannert Pavilion opened in October 1970. Called "a stage-setting for the beautiful" by *Interior Design Magazine*, the new building and the increasingly high-quality art collection it contained received very positive local and national reviews.

In anticipation of its new home, the Art Association's board voted to change the name of the organization to the Indianapolis Museum of Art. This shift signaled the institution's growing ambition to build a truly important art collection and to operate at a level equal to the best art museums in the country. Fortuitously, the new building set within a garden did launch the museum into a phase of fast-paced growth. During this period numerous collectors, including the Krannerts, gave the museum their collections, and attendance reached record highs, which resulted in the need for further expansion. In 1972 the Clowes Pavilion opened as a gift of the family in honor of Edith Whitehill Clowes and as a home for the Clowes Collection of Old Master paintings. A few months later the museum unveiled the arresting Sutphin Fountain in front of the new building. Designed by Sasaki Dawson DeMay Associates of Watertown, Massachusetts, and funded by Sam and Dudley Sutphin as a tribute to their late father, Samuel Brady Sutphin, the circular fountain has become an icon and delights visitors to this day. Expansion continued with the opening of Showalter Pavilion in late 1973. The IMA board had envisioned its new site as a "cultural campus" where art and nature came together and where other arts

above Opening ceremonies for the Herman C. and Ellnora D. Krannert Pavilion, October 25, 1970. Historical Photography Collection (PHO002), IMA Archives.

right Clowes Pavilion opening reception in the courtyard, April 9, 1972. IMA Photography Archives (PHO001), IMA Archives.

far right Fireworks over the Sutphin Fountain during the dedication celebrations on October 25, 1972. The celebration included a dance performance on the fountain itself. *The Indianapolis Star*, October 26, 1972, Publicity Scrapbooks, IMA Archives.

right Dorothy Lynn, who gave the museum $29 million in 1989, February 24, 1965.

far right Winter Nights Film Series screening of *Peter Pan* (1924) in The Tobias Theater, The Toby, 2015.

organizations could partner with the museum. Indianapolis's Civic Theatre took advantage of this vision, and one of its donors, Grace Showalter, funded the construction of a fully functional theater pavilion. For the next 30 years, Civic Theatre called the museum home.

Along with its expanding facility, museum programs and finances grew substantially during the 1970s and 1980s. By 1975, for example, membership had more than tripled to over 12,000. Simultaneously, more dynamic programing was introduced, including the much-loved Summer Nights Film Series, along with affiliate groups whose aim it was to teach people how to collect art and to garden. The museum's conservation program was also founded in the early 1970s and publication efforts expanded. Growth in the endowment and annual support during these years was also noteworthy. At the time of its 100th anniversary in 1983, the endowment was only $37 million. Thanks in part to the success of the newly founded Second Century Society, several large bequests—including $29 million from Dorothy Lynn—and favorable markets, the museum's financial situation was transformed. In less than a decade the endowment grew in value to more than $100 million and in 1989 the first full-master plan was created for the gardens.

The 1990s and 2000s were also decades of great ambition. In 1990 the new Hulman Pavilion opened thanks to a lead gift from Mary Fendrich Hulman. Designed by the well-known American architect Edward Larrabee Barnes of New York, the new building was constructed to house a 1,200-piece collection of African and Oceanic art given by Harrison Eiteljorg, a longtime chairman of the museum's board. In addition, more space was gained for the display of European art, including the Holliday Collection of Neo-Impressionist painting, and a new, state-of-the-art temporary exhibition gallery. Other milestone events during this era were the acquisition of the Josefowitz Collection of works by Paul Gauguin and other Pont-Aven School artists, and the 1999 acquisition of 75 rare and important hanging scrolls and folding screens from Japan's Edo period (1615–1868).

Special exhibitions became more of a focal point at the Indianapolis Museum of Art as well. Shows like *The William S. Paley Collection* (1992); *Gifts of the Tsars 1500–1700: Treasures from the Kremlin* (2001–2002); and *Roman Art from the Louvre* (2008) featured splendid works of art and captured the public's attention. To this day they are among the highest-attended exhibitions ever held at the museum. Education programs and community outreach similarly were advanced in the form of classes for all ages, tours and art camps for schoolchildren, film series, lectures, concerts, and public festivals. The museum's first website was created in 1995 and is now visited by individuals from around the globe. The Stout Reference Library continued to grow, and The Damon C. and Kay D. Davis Lab for interactive learning and the Indianapolis Star Family Studio for children's education were created. A growing annual fund and endowment supported such activities, which in 1997 received a huge boost in the form of a $40-million bequest from Enid Smith Goodrich.

above Aerial view of The Virginia B. Fairbanks Art & Nature Park: 100 Acres, 2015.

facing page Aerial view of Oldfields–Lilly House & Gardens, 2015.

Emboldened by success, the museum updated its master plan in the late 1990s to include the restoration of Lilly House and its original gardens, an art and nature park, and programs that engaged a wide and diverse audience with art and nature experiences. Although it had been given the Oldfields estate in the late 1960s, and some restoration work had been done on the house and gardens, the IMA had not as yet embraced the property's full potential. Realizing that restoring the estate to its former glory would likely draw more visitors and provide countless educational and recreational opportunities, the museum launched a major improvement effort that resulted in Oldfields–Lilly House & Gardens being declared a National Historic Landmark in 2004.

The realization of the Virginia B. Fairbanks Art & Nature Park similarly took several decades. Soon after the Indianapolis Museum of Art was given the Oldfields property and decided to move there

from its old location on 16th Street, local contracting firm Huber, Hunt and Nichols gave 96 acres of land to the west of the museum and gardens. Thoughts about how to best use the former gravel quarry located in a bend of the White River germinated slowly until the late 1990s, when the idea of developing an art and nature park was born. In 2003 Edward Blake of The Landscape Studio in Hattiesburg, Mississippi, and Marlon Blackwell of Marlon Blackwell Architects in Fayetteville, Arkansas, were selected to design the project. Besides the architects, the park's development included much staff, board, and community involvement. A host of donors made the project possible, with the lead gift of $15 million coming from the Richard M. Fairbanks Foundation in memory of Mr. Fairbanks's second wife, Virginia B. Fairbanks, who loved gardens and nature.

Fairbanks Park was not the only large expansion project that took shape during the early 2000s. Feeling now that the grand staircase leading up to the original 1970s-era building was unwelcoming, and desiring more space for galleries, special exhibitions, public

programming, a restaurant, and retail, the staff and board launched a campaign for "The New IMA" in 2001. This effort resulted in a $74 million expansion and renovation project that included architectural elements like the Efroymson Family Entrance Pavilion designed to feel more accessible and inclusive to the public. Jonathan R. Hess of the Indianapolis-based firm Browning Day Mullins Dierdorf was the lead architect. Besides the new entrance pavilion, highlights of his work included the spacious Deer Zink Special Events Pavilion, made possible through a lead gift from Randolph H. Deer and Wayne P. Zink; the Pulliam Family Great

. . . .

above Installation view of *Richard Wentworth: False Ceiling—Indianapolis*, September 25, 2015–September 4, 2016, in the Efroymson Family Entrance Pavilion.

facing page View of the entrance to the Indianapolis Museum of Art at Newfields.

overleaf, left The Randolph Deer and Wayne Zink Special Events Pavilion.

overleaf, right Family Day celebration of Chinese New Year in the Pulliam Family Great Hall, held in partnership with the Asian Art Society, February 7, 2015.

Hall, funded by Myrta J. Pulliam, Deborah Pulliam, and Russell Pulliam in memory of their parents; and the Wood Gallery Pavilion, funded with a lead gift from Richard and Billie Lou Wood. Outside, the institution was also transformed in many ways, especially through the addition of the Sutphin Mall, the largest green roof in Indiana. Upon their completion in 2005, the new additions brought the main museum building up to 677,000 sq. ft., making it physically one of the largest museum facilities in the country.

Also adding to the scale and diversity of the visitor experience was the acquisition of two additional historic estates during the 2000s. In 2000, longtime supporter Allen W. Clowes died and left his family home to the institution for use as a director's residence. Westerley House and Garden, located in the historic Golden Hill neighborhood near the Newfields campus, features a 1922 structure on 5.5 acres. To the south in Columbus, Indiana, is the Miller House and Garden. Completed in 1953 as the home for J. Irwin Miller and Xenia Simons, this property resulted from the exceptional collaboration of three giants in their fields. Eero Saarinen designed the house, Alexander Girard the interiors, and Dan Kiley the gardens. The result is one of the most important Modernist residences in the world, which four of the Miller's children donated over the course of 2009 and 2010.

Because it features a museum, gardens, and park, along with two historic estates, in 2017 the board voted to give a name to the entire

above Westerley House and Garden, 2015.

facing page Miller House and Garden, Columbus, Indiana, 2012.

152-acre campus. By choosing "Newfields" it is hoped that the public will realize that there is an extraordinary range of experience here—a true place for nature and the arts.

Where else can guests enjoy great art and engaging programming, along with dining and shopping? . . . refresh themselves in a 52-acre garden lush with trees, flowers, an orchard, and fountains? . . . explore a 100-acre art and nature park featuring a 35-acre lake, a nineteenth-century canal, the White River, a great meadow, native woods, and contemporary art? . . . and pass back in time by visiting a diverse art collection or three historic estates that range in style from refined classicism to Mid-Century Modern? The answer is ONLY AT NEWFIELDS, a jewel in the heart of Indiana.

the collections and collectors

SINCE ITS FOUNDING IN 1883, THE INDIANAPOLIS MUSEUM OF Art has collected art from around the world. Today the collection contains more than 55,000 works, spanning 5,000 years of human creativity. But beyond the statistics, the story of the museum and its collections is a story of people who believed that nurturing artists and bringing art to the citizens of Indianapolis and the region made for a better, richer, and more rewarding quality of life. This belief has been passed down from one generation to the next, and it continues to inspire the efforts of those who hold the institution in trust today.

Like most great art museums in the United States, the vast majority of artworks in the collection were gifts from individuals. Through the decades, exceptional objects have been donated by collectors throughout America and from abroad. Important private collections that have found a permanent home in the Museum include: The Eliza M. and Sarah L. Niblack Collection of textiles, the Eli Lilly Collection of Chinese art, the Kurt F. Pantzer Collection of works by British artist J. M. W. Turner, the Mrs. and Mrs. Herman C. Krannert collection of European paintings, the W. J. Holliday Collection of Neo-Impressionist paintings, the Harrison and Sonja Eiteljorg Collection of African art, the Colonel Jeff W. Boucher Collection of Baluchi rugs, the Steven Conant Collection of works on paper, and the Marilyn and Eugene Glick Collection of contemporary studio glass. These and many others have left their imprint on the IMA. The Clowes Collection has been exhibited since 1972 in the Clowes Pavilion and is being gifted to the Museum over time by The Clowes Fund.

One of the museum's greatest patrons, Caroline Marmon Fesler set out consciously and systematically to acquire important works of art from a variety of periods, not for her private enjoyment,

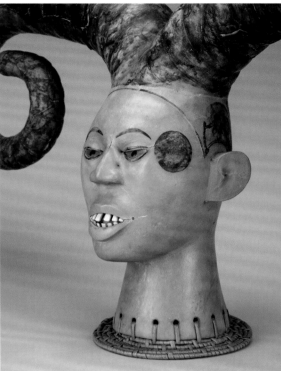

but to enhance the quality of the art holdings the museum could place before the public. In 1944 she wrote to a New York art dealer, "I will tell you what I am trying to do; to build up our small museum by placing these anonymously—as a memorial to my father and mother, some really good pictures—preferably landscapes." With this aim, she purchased and gave to the museum paintings by artists ranging from Cézanne, Van Gogh, Seurat, and Picasso to such seventeenth-century Dutch masters as Hobbema, Cuyp, and Kalf.

The same generous spirit has long animated other individuals and foundations to aid the museum in directly purchasing major works of art for the collection or to establish endowments for that purpose. Since its founding in 1958 the Alliance of the Indianapolis Museum of Art has raised funds in part to support art acquisitions. Similarly, the museum's other affiliate groups that focus on art have helped to develop the collections. Many friends of the museum have contributed to acquisition efforts. Two spectacular examples of such group efforts were the campaigns to acquire the Josefowitz and Strassman collections. During the 1990s the internationally

Strassmans, the Alliance, the Asian Art Society, and many individuals who had established endowment funds for art acquisitions through the years. This great acquisition placed the Indianapolis Museum of Art among a handful of American museums with outstanding collections of Edo-period art. During the late 1990s critical additions to the Neo-Impressionist holdings were made through the generosity of the friends and family of Robert S. Ashby.

The Annual Report of 1907, which appeared a few months after the museum's first permanent building opened, devoted a page to the organization's early "aims and needs":

> *The Art Association proposes to increase its permanent art collection, to hold frequent exhibitions of the production of contemporary American and foreign artists, to develop an art library, to add to the facilities for teaching in the Art School in order to keep abreast of the most advanced methods of instruction, to give lectures, receptions, and entertainments of an artistic character, and in every possible way to encourage the study and love of art among the people.*

The Association's founders would be gratified to know that the museum has held true to its early vision and that it continues to collect, study, and preserve art, to exhibit and interpret it, and to make art accessible to a large and diverse audience. Today the Indianapolis Museum of Art is a treasure house of art from around the globe, including ancient bronze vessels from China, masks of power and beauty from Africa, paintings by the great European and American masters, exquisite objects by eighteenth-century metalsmiths and contemporary studio glass artists, superb rugs from Western Asia, couture fashion of the runways of the world, and contemporary art installations and singular works by living artists.

The museum is more than a storehouse for art, however. It is a community leader in cultural programming and a center of learning for both children and adults. Programming related to the collection, special exhibitions, nature, and human creativity engages thousands of visitors each year. Among the programs are a host of classes, lectures, workshops, tours, and performances. Researchers and the general public use the Stout Art Reference Library, the Horticultural Society Library, and the Archives. There is even an onsite preschool where three-, four-, and five-year-olds learn how art and nature can come together to excite the mind and lift the spirit.

known Swiss collector Samuel Josefowitz became close to the museum and its staff. His exceptional collection of works by Paul Gaugin and other artists from the French Pont-Aven School was of particular interest to the museum, and in 1998 an arrangement was made by which Josefowitz donated part of the collection and the institution purchased the rest. The Lilly Endowment made the acquisition possible by offering an astounding $20 million two-to-one challenge grant that a generous group of private donors matched. In all, 101 works from the Pont-Aven School entered the collection, making Indianapolis home to the finest such collection outside France. Just two years later the museum made another coup with the acquisition of a rare and important group of Japanese paintings assembled by Mr. and Mrs. Alan Strassman. Made during Japan's Edo period (1615–1868) and valued at nearly $10 million at the time, the collection was acquired through the generosity of the

facing page   A school group completes an activity in the Clowes Courtyard, 2016.
Artwork: Bastiano Mainardi (Italian, 1466–1513), *Madonna and Child with
St. Justus of Volterra and St. Margaret of Antioch*, 1507, oil on panel, 63½ × 61 in.
(panel). Gift of Mrs. Booth Tarkington in memory of her husband, 51.58.

above   Guests interact with a Momoyama-period Japanese *attendant bodhisattva*,
about 1575, lacquer on wood, H: 71 in. Gift of Mr. and Mrs. Sidney D. Eskenazi,
Gift of Mr. and Mrs. Irwin Katz, 75.771.

Asian Art

From its beginning in the late nineteenth century, the Indianapolis Museum of Art has collected the art of Asia. Early in the twentieth century, Charles Freer, founder of the Freer Gallery of Asian art in Washington, DC, gave the museum several Asian works of art. Since those early days, generous donors—in the city and elsewhere—have continued to enrich its holdings. Of special note have been the efforts of the museum's Asian Art Society, which was founded by enthusiasts in 1976. Although the collection includes works from all parts of the continent, the Chinese and Japanese holdings are of particular importance, recognized internationally for their outstanding breadth and quality.

The Chinese Collection

China is about the size of Europe and has many regional styles that developed over the course of 6,000 years. The museum has exquisite examples that represent the finest of its traditions in all materials. The bronzes include intricately cast ritual vessels of the Shang and Zhou dynasties (about 1600–256 BCE), mirrors, utilitarian objects, and miniature Buddhist figures. The strongest area of the collection is ceramics, for it includes excellent examples from all periods of Chinese history. Beginning with the middle of the

facing page Tang dynasty (Chinese), *tomb guardian* (detail), early 700s, earthenware with lead glaze, ink and gold, approximately 42⅛ × 19 × 9 in. Anonymous Art Fund, 1997.1.

above Wang Meng (Chinese, about 1308–1385), *Retreat at the Foot of Mt. Hui* (detail), 1320–1385, ink on paper, 11⅝ × 29⅛ in. (image) 11⅝ × 222½ in. (overall). Gift of Mr. and Mrs. Eli Lilly, 60.50.

Neolithic (about 4500 BCE), the encyclopedic collection displays the wonderful achievements of past masters. Tomb figures and vessels capture the diversity of forms and shapes. From the bold, powerful forms and tri-color glazes of the Tang dynasty (618–907 CE), to the elegant and delicate wares of the Song dynasty (960–1279 CE) and the brilliant porcelains of the Ming and Qing dynasties (1368–1911 CE), the accomplishments and changing tastes of regions and times are available for all to see.

The painting collection is rich with important works that document the wide variety of styles and traditions in Chinese art. Particularly noteworthy are works from the academic traditions of the Southern Song dynasty (1127–1279 CE); early artists of the Yuan dynasty (1279–1368 CE), such as Li Kan and Wang Meng, who helped establish the great scholar-painter tradition; later masters such as Shen Zhou and the eccentric Wu Wei of the Ming dynasty (1368–1644 CE); and the academic and orthodox artists, such as "the Four Wangs" of the Qing dynasty (1644–1911 CE).

Crystal, glass, and ivory objects, lacquer ware, furniture, prints, textiles, and sculptures of stone and wood are also part of the collection, which along with the museum's great holding of ceramics, jades, and paintings, make its Chinese collection one of the finest in the United States.

The Japanese Collection

Major achievements in Japanese ceramics, painting, and sculpture from prehistoric times to the present, are contained in the Indianapolis Museum of Art's collection. Virtually all types of Japanese art are available for display, from the religious to the secular, from minute boxes and toggles (*inrō* and *netsuke*) to large-scale Buddhist statues, from refined and subtle objects used in the tea ceremony to those for sumptuous display. The masters Utagawa Hiroshige and Utagawa Kunisada are particularly well represented in the substantial collection of *ukiyo-e* woodblock prints and books that so accurately capture daily life in the Edo period (1600–1868 CE). The works of contemporary ceramists, many of whom Japan has declared Living National Treasures, are also represented in the collection, while beautiful textiles similarly delight the eye.

However, it is Japanese painting for which that the museum is internationally known. In 1904 the very first artworks from Japan entered the collection with the purchase of three contemporary paintings by Nakagawa Hachirō. Since then the collection has come to hold a wide variety of paintings in both screen and scroll formats that illustrate the breadth and richness of that art form in Japan, from examples in purely native styles to those influenced by Chinese and European painting. The most important acquisition of all in this area was made in 2000. That year the museum acquired 75 exceptional works of art from Japan's Edo period, primarily from the collection of Mr. and Mrs. Alan Strassman in Boston. The stars of the group are 20 gloriously painted screens that include depictions of a field of tall grasses glowing gold in the moonlight, corpulent gods wrestling, evocative scenes from *The Tales of Genji*, wild dancing in the streets near a teahouse, and a Noh theater performance in an aristocrat's courtyard. With representative masterworks from nearly all of the major schools of painting from the Edo period, the acquisition transformed the museum's collection into one of the most comprehensive holdings of Edo-period paintings in the United States.

Guests view objects in the exhibition *Tradition Reborn: Contemporary Japanese Ceramics*, July 31, 2015–September 18, 2016, in the Valeria J. Medveckis Gallery.

above Edo period (Japanese), *Monkey with Magnifying Glass,* about 1850, stained ivory, H: 1½ in. Gift of Mr. Edward Petri in memory of Frances Helene Petri, 69.46.65.

right Katsushika Hokusai (Japanese, 1760–1849), *Fine Wind, Clear Morning (Gaifū kaisei)* from the series *Thirty-six Views of Mt. Fuji (Fugaku sanjūrokkei),* about 1800–1849, color woodblock print, 10⅛ × 15 in. Carl H. Lieber Memorial Fund, 60.12.

left Suzuki Sansei (Japanese, b. 1936), *celadon globular jar*, about 1990–1995,
stoneware with cracked powder blue celadon glaze, 14½ × 15⅝ (diam.) in.
(overall). Purchased with funds provided by Leonard and Kathryn Betley,
2009.291.

above left Guests view objects in the exhibition *Tradition Reborn: Contemporary
Japanese Ceramics*, July 31, 2015–September 18, 2016, in the Valeria J. Medveckis
Gallery.

above right School of Tawaraya Sōtatsu (Japanese), *Flowers and Butterflies*
(detail), 1730–1770, ink, color, gold leaf on paper, 51¾ × 123 in. (overall). Mr. and
Mrs. William R. Spurlock Fund, 2005.4.

African Art

Africa is the world's second-largest continent and the cradle of humankind. Known for an abundance of natural resources, Africa is home to deserts, equatorial forests, savannahs, mountain ranges, and wetlands. The great Sahara Desert divides the continent both physically and culturally. In the region north of the Sahara, Islam has had a vast, centuries-old influence. In sub-Saharan Africa, most of the hundreds of languages are related to one another. Despite immense cultural and religious diversity, traditional belief systems among Africans share many significant connections because of these two great historic influences. The Indianapolis Museum of Art's collection of African art celebrates the beauty and richness of these links, and is one of the most encyclopedic African collections in American museums, representing all major art-producing regions of the continent.

Its greatest strength is art from western Africa, with significant holdings from the Yoruba people and the Benin Kingdom of Nigeria. Included are ritual masks and figures and symbols of leadership, notably crowns, articles of dress, and stools. Not only does it include a wide range of examples within the classical corpus of figurative masks and figure sculptures from west and central Africa, it comprises important and extensive holdings of northern, eastern, and southern African arts—areas that until recently were largely ignored by American art museums. The fact that the museum's collection also contains a number of significant contemporary works of African art, including works by artists such as Twins Seven-Seven and Nicholas Mukomberanwa, also places it among the most complete and forward-looking museum collections. Similarly, the presence at the Indianapolis Museum of Art of a large and diverse number of textiles from the African continent further enhances the collections' encyclopedic nature.

· ·

above left Songye people, *community power figure* (detail), early 20th century, wood, cloth, feathers, fur, reptile skin, metals, pigment, H: 33 in. The Ballard Fund, Lucille Stewart Endowed Art Fund, E. Hardey Adriance Fine Arts Acquisition Fund in memory of Marguerite Hardey Adriance, Roger G. Wolcott Fund and Mary V. Black Art Endowment Fund, 2005.21.

left Guests view objects in the Eiteljorg Suite of African Art, 2012.

facing page Installation view of the Eiteljorg Suite of African Art, 2012.

HARRISON EITELJORG

No collector shaped the African collection more than Harrison Eiteljorg, who served as board chair from 1974 to 1983. Raised in a home that appreciated art, Eiteljorg was enrolled in classes at the Indianapolis Museum of Art's precursor, the John Herron Art Institute. In time he went into the advertising business and became involved in coal mining. During his adulthood, Eiteljorg developed an appreciation for non-Western art. In 1965 after purchasing his first piece of African Art from a dealer he was introduced to Dr. Roy Sieber at Indiana University in Bloomington, IN, the father of African studies in America. Over the next decades Sieber helped direct Eiteljorg with his collection. Eiteljorg and his wife, Sonja, donated this collection to the museum in 1989 and provided funds for galleries that carry their names. They also established the Eiteljorg Museum of American Indians and Western Art in Indianapolis to house their extensive Native American and Western collection.

••

facing page Twins Seven-Seven (Nigerian, 1944–2011), *Healing of Abiku Children* (detail), 1973, pigment on wood, carved, 51⅜ × 51⁹⁄₁₆ in. Gift of Mr. and Mrs. Harrison Eiteljorg, 1993.82.

right Fang people, *female figure*, late 19th to early 20th century, wood, fiber, glass, brass, 9¾ × 3 × 3 in. Gift of Mr. and Mrs. Harrison Eiteljorg, 1989.1029.

European Painting and Sculpture

Among this collection are many of the Indianapolis Museum of Art's finest and most important works of art. While the museum's holdings of European art include pieces from the twelfth century to the present, the greatest strengths are seventeenth-century Dutch and Flemish paintings, eighteenth-century French, Italian and British paintings, nineteenth-century paintings and works on paper from the French Pont-Aven School, and works by French and Belgian Neo-Impressionists. To a large extent these highpoints reflect the tastes of several important private collectors who greatly influenced the museum's presentation of European art.

European Art before 1800

The collection includes rare and important examples of fresco painting in two scenes from the life of Christ created around 1125 for the remote Spanish hermitage of San Baudelio de Berlanga.

The range of Italian Renaissance painting is suggested in the stylistic distance between Barnaba de Modena's powerfully expressionistic *Crucifixion*, dating from around 1375, and the humanist naturalism of Titian's *Portrait of a Man*, painted about 125 years later. Renaissance artists outside Italy produced works of comparable quality; among the examples in Indianapolis is the beautiful and miraculously well-preserved *Annunciation Triptych*, painted in Bruges around 1483 by the Master of the Legend of St. Ursula.

The museum's outstanding collection of seventeenth-century Dutch and Flemish painting includes a noteworthy group of landscapes by Meindert Hobbema, Jacob van Ruisdael, Jan van Goyen, Jan Both, and Aelbert Cuyp. Cuyp's *The Valkof at Nijmegen* is one of the artist's finest works. The collection also includes a small but important group of Dutch still-life paintings. Works by seventeenth-century Flemish artists include a self-portrait by Rembrandt van Rijn and one of Anthony van Dyck's earliest works, *The Entry of Christ into Jerusalem,* painted in about 1618.

· ·

Aelbert Cuyp (Dutch, 1620–1691), *The Valkof at Nijmegen* (detail), about 1652–1654, oil on panel, 19¼ × 29 in. Gift in commemoration of the 60th anniversary of the Art Association of Indianapolis in memory of Daniel W. and Elizabeth C. Marmon, 43.107.

The Baroque art of Italy is exemplified by the Caravaggesque naturalism of Valentin de Boulogne's masterful portrayal of Rafaello Menicucci as well as by the stylistically antithetical late Roman classicism of Carlo Maratta's graceful and radiantly colored *Rebecca and Eliezer at the Well*. The advent of the Baroque style in Spain is signaled by Gaspar Núñez Delgado's *Crucifixion,* a work characterized by its robust realism and profoundly human expression of anguish. It is among the most important works of Spanish baroque sculpture in America.

A fine collection of eighteenth-century French paintings by Rococo masters such as Antoine Watteau, François Boucher, and Jean Honoré Fragonard complements the museum's holdings of contemporaneous work by Italian and British artists. The art of eighteenth-century Italy is well represented in turbulent landscapes by Alessandro Magnasco and Marco Ricci, a Venetian *vedute* by Canaletto, imaginary Roman views by Panini, and a splendid oil sketch by Corrado Giaquinto. The extravagant and ingenious art of eighteenth-century France can be seen in Watteau's rustic *Country Dance* and Boucher's more refined *Idyllic Landscape with Woman Fishing.* Only slightly later, Richard Wilson's *Apollo and the Seasons* (about 1768) exemplifies the early picturesque landscape in England.

facing page Rembrandt van Rijn (Dutch, 1606–1669), *Self-Portrait* (detail), about 1629, oil on panel, 17½ × 13½ × ¾ in. (panel). Courtesy of The Clowes Fund, C10063.

right Gaspar Núñez Delgado (Spanish, 1551–1617), *Crucifix*, 1599, ivory, ebony, mahogany, silver, polychromy, 26¾ × 14 × 3¼ in. Gift of Walter E. and Tekla B. Wolf by exchange, 1995.24.

THE CLOWES FAMILY AND WESTERLEY

Between 1931 and the early 1960s, Dr. George H. A. Clowes (1877–1958) and his wife, Edith Whitehill Clowes (1885–1967), built a significant collection of Old Master paintings. British by birth and a medical researcher by profession, Dr. Clowes proved to be an astute art connoisseur, acquiring works by leading European artists like Lucas Cranach the Elder, El Greco, Claude Lorrain, Rembrandt van Rijn, Jusepe de Ribera, and Peter Paul Rubens. The funds to support such major acquisitions came from Dr. Clowes's work at Indianapolis-based pharmaceutical manufacturer Eli Lilly and Company, where he was director of research from 1919 to 1946. His efforts there were the foundation of the family's wealth, providing the means to acquire a fine collection and to house it at Westerley, the family's home in Indianapolis.

Westerley House and Garden was originally built by Josephine Doud Frawley. Situated on rolling property overlooking the Indiana Central Canal, the Italianate mansion was designed by local architect Frederick Wallick. Frawley engaged the well-known, Chicago-based landscape architect Jens Jensen to surround the home with beautiful gardens. In the early 1930s, Dr. Clowes purchased the estate. The home was remodeled in the English Tudor style and expanded to 20 rooms, while more property was acquired to enlarge the gardens to five and a half acres. The Clowes family named their home "Westerley" as a counterpoint to "Easterley," their summer place in Massachusetts.

In 1934 Clowes joined the museum's Board and his influence was quickly felt, as the institution moved more seriously to collect Old Master European paintings. By the time of Dr. Clowes's death in 1958, the family's collection contained 85 Flemish, Italian, Dutch, Spanish, and English works that spanned the fourteenth to the nineteenth centuries. Edith Clowes and her son Allen

continued making important acquisitions and placed them in a private foundation called The Clowes Fund. In 1960 Edith Clowes decided to open her home to guided tours of the family's paintings, which were shown at Westerley to great effect. It was Mrs. Clowes's dream to transform Westerley House and Garden into a museum following her death, but that proved impractical, and the family agreed to transfer the collection to the Indianapolis Museum of Art. Edith Clowes died in 1967, and in her memory her sons Allen and George provided $1 million towards the construction of a building to house the collection at the new site. The Clowes Pavilion opened in early 1972 and has been a favorite part of the museum ever since. In 1999 The Clowes Fund began giving the museum title to its paintings, a process that will be completed in 2021. Beyond donating the collection, The Clowes Fund also annually supports research and conservation on the works of art and the maintenance of the Clowes Pavilion. Upon his death in 2000, Allen Clowes bequeathed Westerley House and Garden to serve as the director's residence and as a gracious place to host receptions.

above left Installation view of the Clowes Courtyard, 2013.

above right Interior period view of Westerley House.

facing page Jusepe de Ribera (Spanish, 1590–1652), *Aristotle* (detail), 1637, oil on canvas, 49 x 39 in. The Clowes Collection, 2000.245.

European Painting and Sculpture, 1800–1945

From the dramatic landscapes of J.M.W. Turner to the geometric forms of Fernand Léger's machine age, the nineteenth- and twentieth-century European painting collection includes many of the Indianapolis Museum of Art's best-loved works. The collection's earlier paintings draw upon the harmony and order of the Neoclassical movement or the Romantic era's fascination with nature. The Barbizon School of mid-nineteenth-century France lives on through the landscapes of Corot, Daubigny, and Millet; while vivid canvases by Renoir and Pissarro exemplify the brilliant color and luminous effects of French Impressionism. Late-career views of London and Venice demonstrate Monet's long-standing commitment to the movement.

below A young guest views Jean-Pierre Feuillet (French, 1777–1840), *vase*, about 1825, hard paste porcelain, polychrome enamels, gilding, H: 18 in. Mr. and Mrs. William Spurlock and Lilly Pavilion Discretionary Funds, 1988.221.

facing page Joseph Mallord William Turner (English, 1775–1851), *East Cowes Castle, the Seat of J. Nash, Esq., the Regatta Beating to Windward*, 1828, oil on canvas, 35½ × 47½ in. Gift of Mr. and Mrs. Nicholas Noyes, 71.32.

At the heart of the museum's superb Post-Impressionist collection are three magnificent canvases by Cézanne, Van Gogh, and Gauguin, working at the height of their powers. The museum also possesses the finest group of paintings by Georges Seurat and his Neo-Impressionist followers outside Europe. This unique collection documents the development and impact of the Neo-Impressionist movement (sometimes also referred to as Pointillist) from the 1880s through the early years of the twentieth century, featuring canvases by many of the movement's key figures. One of the collection's distinctions is its unusual strength in rare works by the Belgian and Dutch Neo-Impressionists.

With the acquisition of 101 works in 1998, the museum's Pont-Aven School holdings moved from zero to the largest and finest in the country. The 17 paintings and 84 prints were created by Paul Gauguin and an international group of progressive artists working in Brittany, on the western coast of France, during the 1880s and '90s. Works by Emile Bernard, Paul Sérusier, Maurice Denis, and Jan Verkade can be seen in the gallery devoted to the School. Paintings by Édouard Vuillard, Odilon Redon, Georges Lacombe and other artists associated with the Symbolist movement also have a distinct presence in the European galleries. Together with the Neo-Impressionist collection, they offer an unparalleled view of the beginning of modern painting.

Cubism, one of the first really pivotal movements of the twentieth century, is represented by the canvases of Picasso and Braque. Figural and landscape paintings by Modigliani and Dufy exemplify the artists affiliated with the School of Paris, when the French capital was the center of the Western art world. While a signature Léger canvas assumes the machine-like forms of the modern era, works by Chagall, Rouault, and De Chirico turn to whimsical, spiritual, or surreal themes.

The museum's nineteenth-century sculpture collection ranges from French *animalier* bronzes to Romantic works by Feuchère and Carpeaux to expressive, tormented figures by Auguste Rodin and George Minne. As for the twentieth century, an intriguing variety of images of women moves from the pathos of German Expressionism to the classicism of Aristide Maillol and Joseph Bernard to the elegant abstraction of Alexander Archipenko.

• •

Vincent van Gogh (Dutch, 1853–1890), *Landscape at Saint-Rémy (Enclosed Field with Peasant)*, 1889, oil on canvas, 30 × 37½ in. Gift of Mrs. James W. Fesler in memory of Daniel W. and Elizabeth C. Marmon, 44.74.

above Pablo Picasso (Spanish, 1881–1973), *Ma Jolie*, 1913–1914, oil on canvas,
21³⁄₁₆ × 25⅝ in. Bequest of Mrs. James W. Fesler, 61.36.

facing page Henry van de Velde (Belgian, 1863–1957), *Père Biart Reading in
the Garden* (detail), 1890 or 1891, oil on brown paper mounted to canvas,
24⁷⁄₁₆ × 20⁷⁄₁₆ in. The Holliday Collection, 79.320.

CAROLINE MARMON FESLER

Fesler counts among the museum's most generous and discerning patrons. Born in 1878, she was the daughter of the founder of the Marmon Motor Car Company and the owner of the manufacturing concern Mordyke & Marmon Co. of Indianapolis. She studied at Smith College and in Paris and developed an abiding love for art and music. At age 39, she married Indianapolis lawyer James Fesler.

    Caroline Fesler was highly involved with the growing museum and art school, becoming its president in 1942. From that time until her death in 1960, Fesler built a stellar collection of European paintings for the museum. She had an uncanny ability to sense greatness, and her taste was expansive, ranging from seventeenth-century Dutch landscapes to twentieth-century Modernist art. Her first gifts included paintings by Dutch and French masters. Fesler also challenged the conservatism of the museum's board by acquiring and offering startlingly modern pictures as well. Avant-garde art was still difficult for some at the museum to accept at the time. In 1944 the museum's Fine Arts Committee declined to acquire Picasso's 1914 Cubist painting, Ma Jolie. It was subsequently purchased by Fesler and bequeathed to the museum upon her death, along with canvases by Braque and Chagall.

W. J. HOLLIDAY

Created by Georges Seurat and his followers in the 1880s, the Neo-Impressionist or Pointillist movement used recent discoveries in color behavior to create striking images through the juxtaposition of small dots of paint on canvas. W. J. (Jack) Holliday, a prominent patron, ensured that the museum would hold one of the world's finest collections of Neo-Impressionist art.

    Holliday was the chairman of W. J. Holliday & Co., a steel warehousing and sales firm, as well as vice-chairman of Monarch Steel Co. While he originally collected American art and rare books, in the 1950s Holliday began purchasing European paintings in Paris and New York. With advice from dealer friends to focus his collecting on a specific area, Holliday turned his attention to the work of Georges Seurat and his followers in the Neo-Impressionist movement. Between 1957 and 1971, he traveled extensively in pursuit of Pointillist works and acquired 96 paintings by 85 artists. To celebrate Holliday's achievement the Indianapolis Museum of Art mounted an exhibition of the collection in 1971 that inspired the collector to bequeath the works to it upon his death in 1977. The result is an internationally respected Neo-Impressionist collection that is the finest in America.

SAMUEL JOSEFOWITZ

In 1886 Gauguin made the first of several visits to the Pont-Aven region, where he was attracted by the inexpensive cost of living, picturesque countryside, and romantic appeal of Breton traditions. Working with his young colleague Émile Bernard during the summer of 1888, he developed an approach to painting that favored imagination and the expressive potential of line, color, and pattern, rather than the efforts to copy nature. The results were works that became precursors of abstraction.

During the 1950s and '60s, Swiss businessman and collector Samuel Josefowitz formed a major collection of Pont-Aven works before the movement's significance was widely recognized. "I was attracted by the experimental quality of this art—the sense that it was a new way of painting," he said in a 1999 interview. "My interest in the Pont-Aven School was like a voyage of discovery. As I began to collect these works, each acquisition was like the discovery of a new world." Josefowitz bought pieces not only by the movement's two founders, but also by their followers, assembling the world's finest collection in private hands. With the gift and acquisition of his collection, the Indianapolis Museum of Art became a global leader in the study of Paul Gauguin and the artists of the Pont-Aven School.

••

Paul Gauguin (French, 1848–1903), *The Flageolet Player on the Cliff*, 1889, oil on canvas, 27^{15}⁄$_{16}$ × 35^{15}⁄$_{16}$ in. Samuel Josefowitz Collection of the School of Pont-Aven, through the generosity of Lilly Endowment Inc., the Josefowitz Family, Mr. and Mrs. James M. Cornelius, Mr. and Mrs. Leonard J. Betley, Lori and Dan Efroymson, and other Friends of the Museum, 1998.168.

Paul Manship
American, 1885–1966

The Flight of Europa 1925
gilt bronze on agate base

Gift of Lucy M. Taggart in memory of her brother
Thomas D. Taggart
81.46

- Manship achieves a witty interpretation of the classical myth of Europa, a woman abducted by Zeus. The god transformed himself into a bull to carry her across the sea.

- The rhythmic composition sets horizontal against vertical and speed versus stillness, as the bull's horns, tail, and legs oppose Europa's upright stance.

American Painting and Sculpture

Throughout the Indianapolis Museum of Art's history, American art and artists have played prominent roles in the life of the institution. In its early years, the famous Indiana artist T. C. Steele served as chairman of the Fine Arts Committee. While Steele assisted the museum in acquiring art for its young collection, his colleagues J. Ottis Adams and William Forsyth taught painting in the art school. Collecting the work of these and other artists of the so-called Hoosier School has always been a special interest, and the museum now has the finest collection of art by early Indiana artists in the country.

The museum's early efforts laid a strong foundation for future growth. Today its American art holdings range from colonial portraits by Gilbert Stuart to likenesses by Thomas Eakins, William Merritt Chase, and John Singer Sargent. The grandeur and beauty of the American landscape can be seen in panoramic Hudson River School views and the mystic reveries of George Inness and the

···

left Installation view of Paul Manship (American, 1885–1966), *The Flight of Europa*, 1925, gilt bronze on agate base, 25 × 30½ × 8¼ in. Gift of Lucy M. Taggart in memory of her brother, Thomas D. Taggart, 50.30.

below Installation view of the Andrew and Jane Paine Galleries, 2015.

Tonalists. A small gem by Winslow Homer is one of the department's best-loved works.

American Impressionism has become one of the collection's richest areas. With works by Childe Hassam, J. H. Twachtman, Robert Vonnoh, J. Alden Weir, William Paxton, Edmund Tarbell, Robert Reid, Richard Miller, Louis Ritman, and Frederick Frieseke, the museum can feature the full range of the Impressionist movement as manifested in America.

The Realist, Social Realist, and Regionalist schools active in America during the 1930s and '40s are represented by Thomas Hart Benton, Jacob Lawrence, and Reginald Marsh, as well as two key works by Edward Hopper. The Modernist movement of the same era includes paintings by Marsden Hartley, Arthur Dove, and John Marin, with special strength in the works of Georgia O'Keeffe.

American sculpture has always been of importance to the museum. Its most successful exhibition in the early twentieth century was the *Augustus Saint-Gaudens Memorial Exhibition*. Featuring the work of one of America's finest sculptors, the show was held in late 1909 and early 1910 and set an attendance record that would not be matched for decades. Interest in this area continued, and today the museum's nineteenth-century American sculpture collection ranges from the sober dignity of Neoclassical marble to the playfulness and elegance of bronzes by Frederick MacMonnies and Saint-Gaudens. A strong group of pieces by Paul Manship, John Storrs, and Gaston Lachaise creates a fascinating blend of classical themes and Modernist symbols, all crafted in the midst of the Roaring Twenties.

facing page Edward Hopper (American, 1882–1967), *Hotel Lobby*, 1943, oil on canvas, 32¼ × 40¾ in. William Ray Adams Memorial Collection, 47.4.

left Installation view of Randolph Rogers (American, 1825–1892), *Ruth Gleaning*, modeled 1853, carved 1860, marble on plum marble pedestal, 35½ × 20 × 20 in. Gift in honor of Mr. and Mrs. William L. Fortune by their children and Gift of the Alliance of the IMA, 1988.219.

facing page Richard Emile Miller (American, 1875–1943), *Afternoon Tea* (detail), 1910, oil on canvas, 39½ × 32 in. Gift of Andrew and Jane Paine, 1997.139.

above Georgia O'Keeffe (American, 1887–1986), *Jimson Weed*, 1936, oil on linen, 70 × 83½ in. Gift of Eli Lilly and Company, 1997.131.

overleaf, left Installation view of Augusta Savage (American, 1892–1962), *Gamin*, about 1930, painted plaster, 9⅛ × 5¾ × 4⅛ in. The Indianapolis Chapter of the Links, Inc., Gift of the Friends of American Art by exchange, 2008.183.

overleaf, right Winslow Homer (American, 1836–1910), *The Boat Builders* (detail), 1873, oil on panel, 6 × 10¼ in. Martha Delzell Memorial Fund, 54.10.

Works on Paper

The Indianapolis Museum of Art's largest collection is its more than 22,000 works on paper, including manuscripts, early printed books, prints, photographs, and drawings dating from the fifteenth to the twenty-first centuries. The wide-ranging collection contains the works of many famous artists, including a representative group of Old Master prints and drawings with works by Dürer, Rembrandt, and Goya. Holdings of more modern works include Post-Impressionist prints by Toulouse-Lautrec as well as Modernist examples by Picasso, Matisse, and Chagall. Toulouse-Lautrec's daringly original *Moulin Rouge—La Goulue* (1891) displays the artist's talent for caricature, and was the most important gift of a group known as the Gamboliers, who banded together in the 1930s to purchase works of modern art for the museum. Numerous American artists are also represented, with fine examples by artists ranging from George Wesley Bellows to Andy Warhol.

The museum holds rare examples of drawings by Giambattista Tiepolo, Antoine Watteau, Jean-Auguste Dominique Ingres, Edgar Degas, John Singer Sargent, Winslow Homer, and Isamu Noguchi, along with an array of photographs taken by artists as diverse as William Henry Fox Talbot, Julia Margaret Cameron, Alexander Rodchenko, Brassai, Robert Frank, and Diane Arbus. However, it is the museum's holdings of watercolors, prints, and drawings by Joseph Mallord William Turner, the acclaimed master of English landscape painting, for which its works-on-paper collection is internationally known. Bequeathed to the museum in 1979, it contains 38 watercolors, 3,000 etchings, 7 life portraits, many letters, and 500 books, along with works by some of Turner's contemporaries. When additional pieces by Turner are taken into account, including two major oil paintings, the museum holds one of the world's most comprehensive collections of works by the artist.

facing page Julia Margaret Cameron (British, 1815–1879), *The Rosebud Garden of Girls* (detail), 1868, albumen print, 12¹⁄₁₆ × 10⅝ in. Allen Whitehill Clowes Fund, 1993.16.

right Henri de Toulouse-Lautrec (French, 1864–1901), *Moulin Rouge-La Goulue*, 1891, ink on paper, color lithograph, 67 × 46¾ in. Gift of the Gamboliers, 36.4.

KURT F. PANTZER

Kurt Pantzer discovered the work of nineteenth-century British artist Joseph Mallord William Turner while a law student at Harvard University. As part of his studies, Pantzer learned how Turner was recognized as one of the greatest landscape painters of all time, and how he was considered the father of watercolor painting and a forerunner of modern art in the impressionistic style. Pantzer came to love J. M. W. Turner's closeness to nature and his emphasis on light, atmosphere, and color and vowed to buy an example of the artist's work after he made his first $100,000. His achievement went far beyond that in the end.

The Pantzer family had been involved in the Art Association from its beginnings, and Kurt Pantzer was highly engaged as well. As a lawyer and member of the board, he facilitated the transition from the John Herron Art Institute to the Indianapolis Museum of Art in 1969 and its subsequent relocation to the corner of Michigan Road and 38th Street. Simultaneously, Pantzer was the world's most active collector of Turner's work, which in his great generosity he bequeathed to the museum upon his death.

above left A guest interacting with a label in the exhibition *Gustave Baumann, German Craftsman – American Artist*, October 24, 2015–February 14, 2016, in the Allen Whitehill Clowes Special Exhibition Gallery.

above right Joseph Mallord William Turner (English, 1775–1851), *Venice: The Rialto*, 1820–1821, watercolor over pencil on white paper, 11¼ × 16¼ in. (sheet). Gift in memory of Dr. and Mrs. Hugo O. Pantzer by their children, 72.183.

facing page George Wesley Bellows (American, 1882–1925), *A Stag at Sharkey's* (detail), 1917, ink on paper, lithograph, 18⅝ × 23⅞ in. (image) 21⅜ × 27¾ in. (sheet). Gift of Mrs. George Ball, 26.5

Textile and Fashion Arts

The Indianapolis Museum of Art was one of the first art institutions in the United States to collect textiles. The collection was begun in 1888 and quickly grew. In 1906, over 100 Chinese textiles and costumes were purchased by the museum through the John Herron Fund. By 1915, the collection had grown rapidly in the areas of Chinese, Japanese, European, Persian, and Indian textiles and costumes. It now contains more than 6,000 works that represent virtually all of the world's traditions in fabrics and reveals the dissemination of style and technique among many different cultures. The range of the holdings is truly astonishing—European lace and tapestries, Chinese embroideries and painted silks, American quilts and printed fabrics, Moroccan textiles and rugs, African textiles and masquerade costumes, Japanese kimonos, and couture dresses just off the runways of the world. Among the latter is the Indiana Fashion Design Collection that features fine examples by great designers who are connected to the Hoosier state, including Bill Blass, Roy Halston Frowick, Norman Norell, and Stephen Sprouse. Since 2010 the Fashion Arts Society has supported the expansion of the textile and fashion arts collection and funds a wide range of programs that engage its members and the general public. In addition many private individuals and families have assisted the museum throughout the years in building its textile and fashion collections.

Installation view of *Cutting-Edge Fashion: Recent Acquisitions,* April 17, 2015–January 3, 2016, in the Gerald and Dorit Paul Galleries.

Installation view of *Majestic African Textiles*, May 3, 2013–March 2, 2014, in the Gerald and Dorit Paul Galleries.

THE NIBLACK FAMILY

From the beaches of the South Pacific to the deserts of North Africa, admiral Albert Parker Niblack's 40-year career in the U.S. Navy took him far from his boyhood home in Indiana. Along the way, he not only advanced in rank but also developed an abiding interest in the different cultures he encountered.

Between the early 1880s and his retirement in 1923, Niblack traveled the globe with the Navy and quickly became knowledgeable about many cultural and artistic traditions. His earliest gifts to the museum included significant works of Northwest Coast American Indian art; these were augmented by further gifts of Native American art by his widow upon his passing in 1929.

Niblack's sisters, Eliza and Sarah, were likewise engaged in their brother's passions for travel and textiles and augmented his gifts through the decades. Eliza donated 600 works of art to the museum, and after her untimely death in 1930, 800 additional works were given to it. Her younger sister Sarah inherited the rest of Eliza's textile collection. After Sarah died, her heirs, nieces Narcissa Thorne and Lydia Swith, donated the remaining 2,500-piece textile collection, helping make the Indianapolis Museum of Art a true force in the field.

JEFF W. BOUCHER

Colonel Jeff W. Boucher grew up on a Texas ranch and collected from childhood. In 1951, while stationed in Germany as the commander of a U.S. Army combat engineer battalion, he purchased three Baluchi rugs. These acquisitions incited in him an interest in collecting oriental rugs. In the early 1960s a dealer friend suggested Boucher concentrate on early tribal and nomadic weavings, including those woven by the semi-nomadic Baluchi people who lived in border region between Afghanistan and Iran. Realizing that the Baluchi way of life was threatened by the spread of modern culture, Boucher sought out the best examples of their traditional rugs from the late nineteenth and early twentieth centuries.

Colonel Boucher died in 1994 and his widow, Shirley Boucher, considered donating the collection to various institutions before giving it to the museum in 1996. Ultimately she concluded that Indianapolis's state-of-the-art textile storage facilities, conservation capabilities, accessibility to scholars, and dedicated textile exhibition gallery made the museum the perfect home for her late husband's prized weavings. Her gift of the 98-piece collection, along with a 400-volume library on oriental rugs, instantly catapulted the museum to international stature among rug scholars, collectors, and curators.

••

above right Moroccan, *wall hanging (haiti)* (detail), mid-1800s, silk velvet weave with silk supplementary warp (solid velvet), embroidered with metallic thread, pieced, 66 × 166 in. The Eliza M. and Sarah L. Niblack Collection, 1983.66.

right Baluchi people, *rug* (detail), 1870–1900, wool, 28 × 51 in. Colonel Jeff W. Boucher Collection, 1996.30.

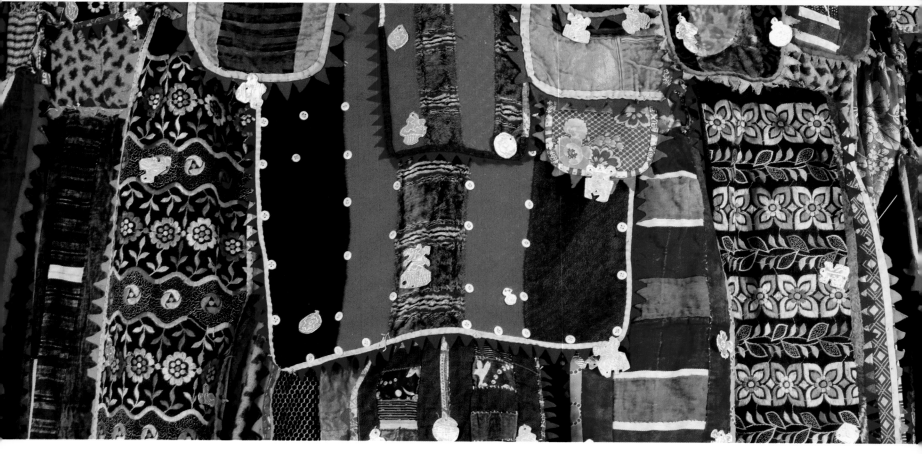

facing page, top left Charles Frederick Worth (English, 1825–1895), *Imperial Russian court dress*, about 1888, silk velvet, silver moire, embroidered with clear glass crystals, silver sequins, silver foil, silver strips. L: 47½ in. (skirt). Gift of the Alliance of the Indianapolis Museum of Art, 2006.3A-C.

facing page, top right Chinese, *Bodhisattva of Wisdom (Mañjusri) (detail)*, 1368–1644, silk, silk and gold wrapped threads, 17⅜ × 7⅝ in. Martha Delzell Memorial Fund, 1992.66.

facing page, bottom Yoruba people, *Egungun masquerade garment (detail)*, 1930–1970, cotton, wool, synthetic fabrics, metal, 68 × 72 in. Costume Fund, 1992.68.

right Halston (American, 1932–1990), *Evening Dress*, 1972, silk knit, 56 × 38 in. Gift of the Alliance of the Indianapolis Museum of Art and purchased with funds provided by Gene and Rosemary Tanner, Patricia J. LaCrosse, Walter and Joan Wolf, Anne Greenleaf, and Frank and Barbara Grunwald, 2010.227.

facing page Portuguese, *oratory commode*, late 18th century, jacaranda wood, gilding, copper alloy, silver, gesso, polychrome, fabric, metal, glass, 124¾ × 56¹¹⁄₁₆ × 27½ in. (installed). Mr. and Mrs. William R. Spurlock Fund, Deaccessioned Decorative Art Fund, Nancy Foxwell Neuberger Acquisition Endowment Fund, Don B. and Suzanne K. Earnhart Art Purchase Fund, Gift of Mrs. Isabelle J. Dixon by exchange, Bequest of Mrs. Herbert Duckwall by exchange, Gift of Dr. Phillip B. Reed in memory of Genevieve Pickerell Reed by exchange, Gift of Mr. and Mrs. J. Irwin Miller by exchange, Gift of Mr. and Mrs. William Ball by exchange, Mr. and Mrs. Eugene C. Pulliam Fund by exchange, Martha Delzell Memorial Fund by exchange, Margaret Mattingly Fund by exchange, Julius F. Pratt Fund by exchange, Margaret Mattingly Fund by exchange, Gift of Mr. and Mrs. J. David Baker by exchange, Gift of Mr. and Mrs. Robert H. Morse, Jr. by exchange, Jacob Metzger Fund by exchange, Jerry M. Wright by exchange, Gift of Mrs. George H. Orndorff by exchange, Lilly Pavilion Discretionary Fund by exchange, Gift in memory of Mrs. Fletcher Hodger by her family by exchange, Gift of Mrs. Florence Schwerin and Ms. Catherine Stace in memory of their mother, Mrs. Peck by exchange, Gift of Ruth Pratt Bobbs and Lois Pratt Knefler by exchange, 2015.66A-G.

above Charles Osborne, designer (American, 1848–1920) for Tiffany & Co. (American, est. 1837), *"Goelet" Racing Cup for Schooners*, 1885, silver, 29 × 13 × 12 in. Gift of a friend of the museum and admirer of its Director, 2016.362.

Design and Decorative Arts

The Indianapolis Museum of Art has collected utilitarian objects that demonstrate excellence in design and technical skill since its founding in 1883. Numerous individual donors have supported this effort, as has the Design Arts Society, which was founded in 1970 to raise funds to purchase new works for the collection and to support educational programs in the field for its members and the general public. The collective work of supporters and curators over more than a century has given the museum broad design and decorative art holdings that sweep across 500 years of human creativity, from the Renaissance to today.

Initially, the institution sought to tell the story of design by building a small, yet high-quality, collection of objects. Using this strategy, the museum has acquired fine ceramics made in important workshops and factories in America, Austria, Britain, France, Germany, and Italy that show the public how styles and production techniques changed over the course of several centuries. Likewise, the furniture collection hits the highpoints of stylistic change, including seventeenth-century Baroque, eighteenth-century Rococo and Neoclassicism, nineteenth-century Neo-Gothic, and early-twentieth-century Art Nouveau. The metalwork collection charts a similar trajectory and features masterpieces by famous craftsmen like the Englishman Paul de Lamerie, the Frenchmen Jean-Baptiste-Claude Odiot and Jean-Valentin Morel, and the Italian Antonio Cortelazzo. Most unusual within the museum's collection are two groups of objects. The first is a significant group of pewter pieces by the German firm J.P. Kayser & Son, made around 1900 and donated by William Swann and William Leazer. The second is the biggest collection in existence of metalwork by the Indianapolis Arts and Crafts designer Janet Payne Bowles, which she created between 1910 and 1930. It was given by her family in her memory.

The museum also collected contemporary design from an early date. For example, in 1917, ceramics recently made by Elizabeth and Hannah Overbeck at their pottery in Indiana were acquired. The gift of the Glick Collection of contemporary glass in the 1990, which traces the 50-year development of the American and International Studio Glass Movements through works by most of the seminal artists from America, Europe, and Asia, greatly advanced the museum's standing in the field.

MARILYN AND EUGENE GLICK

The philanthropic spirit of Marilyn and Eugene Glick manifested itself early on. Their firm, the Gene B. Glick Company, was born out of a young WWII veteran's desire to help his fellow GIs build homes for their families. As their business grew, so did the Glick's desire and ability to help others.

Marilyn Glick had long been a contemporary art enthusiast, but her love for glass was ignited when she visited the Toledo Museum of Art in 1972 and saw its renowned glass collection. From that moment forward, Marilyn Glick dedicated herself to learning more about the contemporary glass movement. Driven by her passion, in the early 1980s the Glicks began to enthusiastically purchase works from the artists they had come to know. By the time of their deaths, the couple had built one of the most expansive collections of contemporary glass in the United States, which they donated to the museum. Because of its large size, the museum has proudly shared the collection with the Marilyn K. Glick Center for Glass at Ball State University in Muncie, Indiana,

above Harvey K. Littleton (American, 1922–2013), *Blue Crown*, 1988, hot worked barium/potash glass with multiple cased overlays of Kugler colors, dimensions vary. Gift of Marilyn and Eugene Glick, 1991.221A-L.

facing page Jean-Baptiste-Claude Odiot (French, 1763–1850), Pierre-Paul Prud'hon, designer (French, 1758–1823), and Adrien-Louis-Marie Cavelier, designer (French, 1785–1867), *soup tureen, cover, and liner from the Branicki Service* (detail), 1819, gilded silver, 21 1/16 × 28 5/8 × 10 3/8 in. Purchased with funds provided by Steve and Tomisue Hilbert, the Marian and Harold Victor Fund, and the Beeler Fund, 1997.139A–C.

Contemporary Industrial Design

In the late 2000s, the Indianapolis Museum of Art dramatically increased its commitment to design by acquiring Miller House and Garden in Columbus, Indiana, and by building a deep collection of contemporary industrial design. As discussed later, the Miller House and Garden is the extraordinary Modernist creation of patrons J. Irwin and Xenia Simons Miller, architect Eero Saarinen, interior designer Alexander Girard, and landscape architect Dan Kiley. It represents a highpoint in mid-twentieth-century design, and can be thought of as the most important masterpiece in the design collection.

In parallel with Miller House and Garden stands the museum's industrial design collection. Since 2008, over 3,000 objects have been collected for a rotating display in dedicated design galleries. Included are innovative examples of furniture, glass, ceramics, metalwork, lighting, and technology design by great designers from Europe, the United States, and Asia like Ron Arad, Maarten Baas, Naoto Fukasawa, Konstantin Grcic, Frank Gehry, Zaha Hadid, Joris Laarman, Ettore Sottsass, Philippe Starck, and Marcel Wanders. While the collection begins in the years following WWII, it focuses most on objects created between 1980 and the present and continues to grow through the addition of newly made works. In sum, the museum's industrial design holdings are one of the largest such collections in any North American art museum, and are among the first surveys of recent trends in this dynamic field.

left Alessandro Mendini (Italian, b. 1931), Atelier Mendini (manufacturer), *Poltrona di Proust lounge chair* (detail), 1978, painted wood and fabric, 42⅝ × 41⅜ × 30 in. Robertine Daniels Art Fund in Memory of Her Late Husband, Richard Monroe Fairbanks Sr., and Her Late Son, Michael Fairbanks, 2013.15.

facing page Installation view of the Contemporary Design Galleries, 2013.

top right Michael Graves (American, 1934–2015), Officina Alessi (manufacturer), *Tea & Coffee Piazza*, designed 1980–1983, made 2010, sterling silver, lacquered aluminum, polyamide, Bakelite, and crystal, 10⅞ × 6⅛ × 6⅛ in. (installed). Gift in honor of Joyce A. Sommers with funds provided by V. Simon Abraham, Cornelius M. and Dorothy Alig, Ruthelen Burns, William J. and Vickie Cafaro, Robert M. Davis, Scott Evenbeck, Russell and Penny B. Fortune, William L. Fortune Jr. and Joseph D. Blakely, Mark M. and Carmen S. Holeman, John David Hoover, Frederick M. King, Kay F. Koch, James E. and Patricia J. LaCrosse, Catharine D. Lichtenauer, Katherine C. Nagler, Nancy J. Ramsey, George J. Seybert, Trent Spence, James A. and Cheryl S. Strain, James P. and Anna S. White, Design Arts Society Fund, 2011.2.1–.5A–C.

bottom right Robert Venturi (American, b. 1925), Venturi Scott Brown and Associates (American, established 1989), and Paul Downs Cabinetmakers (manufacturer), *Louis XVI Lowboy (Chest)*, 1984, painted wood, 30½ × 30 × 18 in. Design Arts Society Fund with funds provided by Dr. Shirley M. Mueller, 2013.1.

facing page Konstantin Grcic (German, b. 1965), Magis S.p.A. (manufacturer), *Chair One*, 2004, die-cast aluminum, polyester powder paint, concrete, A) base: 17½ × 15 (diam.) in. B) seat: 16 × 21½ × 17 in. Gift of Magis S.p.A., 2013.131A–B.

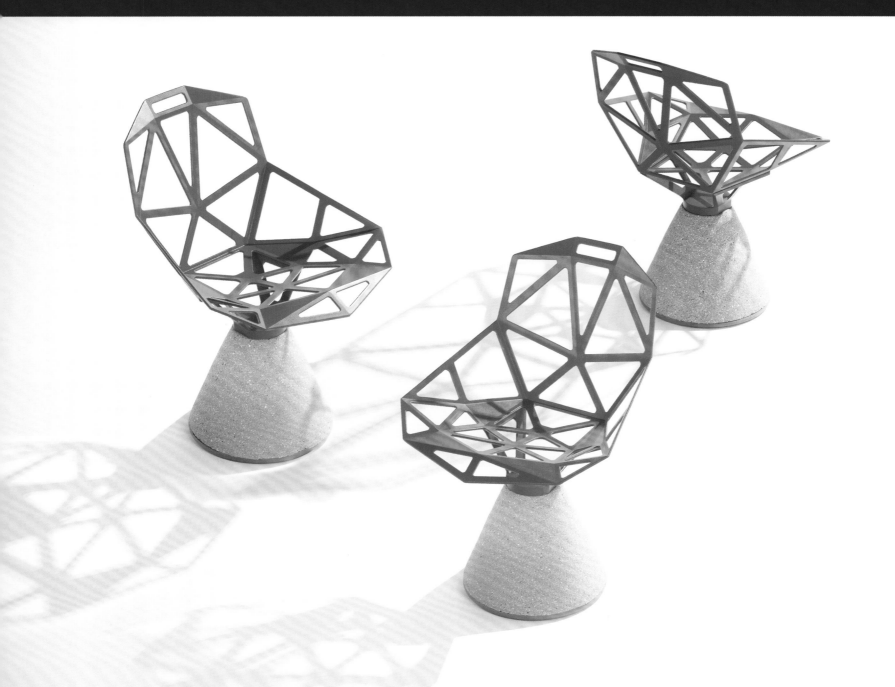

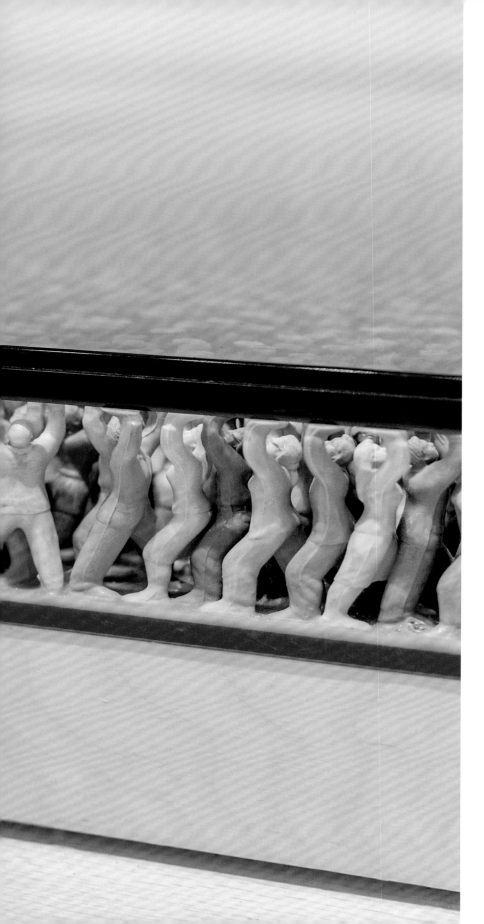

Contemporary Art

The Indianapolis Museum of Art has always collected the work of living artists, and many of its departments hold contemporary treasures. However, the establishment of a separate department for art created after World War II only happened in 1985. Leading up to this momentous step was the founding in 1962 of the Contemporary Art Society (CAS). For over 50 years, CAS has assisted the museum in actively building a contemporary collection, while educating the public and its members through interaction with new art and artists.

Two of the largest groups of contemporary works given to the museum are the Joseph Cantor Collection, consisting primarily of pre-1960 European works and including artists such as Balthus and Antoni Tàpies, and the gifts of Ann M. Stack, which include works by Do-Ho Suh and Joan Mitchell. Notable American works in the museum's contemporary collection include two 1948 paintings by Josef Albers and an Alexander Calder mobile from 1958. Paintings and sculpture by artists from Indiana are another strength of the department. These works include sculptures by David Smith, George Rickey, John Chamberlain, and Bruce Nauman, as well as Robert Indiana's monumental *LOVE* sculpture, which is perhaps the most iconic work in the collection. Since the 1980s, the museum has acquired installations by artists like Robert Irwin, Vito Acconci, James Turrell, Sol LeWitt, and Spencer Finch for display inside the museum. Meanwhile, for display outside on the Sutphin Mall, the museum acquired Roy Lichtenstein's largest sculpture, *Five Brushstrokes*. In addition, with the opening of the Efroymson Family Entrance Pavilion in 2005 and the Virginia B. Fairbanks Art & Nature Park in 2010, the institution has become known for commissioning artists to create new works that purposely engage visitors. These efforts have led to major installations such as Jeppe Hein's *Bench Around the Lake* and Alfredo Jaar's *Park of the Laments,* both of which are now in the permanent collection, as well as a long series of temporary works for the pavilion. Enlivening this wonderful art is a major public programing effort that brings artists and people together. While these efforts focus on Indianapolis and Indiana, in 2011 the museum was honored to represent the United States with the exhibition *Gloria* at the 54th International Art Exhibition in Venice, Italy (La Biennale di Venezia).

facing page Do-Ho Suh (Korean, b. 1962), *Floor* (detail), 1997–2000, PVC figures, glass plates, phenolic sheets, polyurethane resin, 5⅞ × 315¹/₁₆ × 157½ in. (installed). Ann M. Stack Fund for Contemporary Art, 2004.152.

right Joan Mitchell (American, 1925–1992), *Diabolo (neige et fleurs); Diabolo (Snow and Flowers)*, 1969, oil on canvas, 102⅜ × 70¾ in. Gift of Ann M. Stack in honor of Holly Day, former Senior Curator of Contemporary Art, 1998.184.

above left Mark Dion (American, b. 1961), *Harbingers of the Fifth Season*, 2014, mixed media installation featuring watercolors, 62¼ × 120 × 52½ in. (installed). Dedicated to Sherman O'Hara, former IMA Chief Designer, by his friends Ann M. and Chris Stack, 2015.27A-M.4A-L.

left Gregory Crewdson (American, b. 1962), *Untitled*, 1998, chromogenic color print, 47½ × 59½ in. (image). Purchased with funds provided by Kay F. Koch in memory of Bryan B. Molloy, 2006.112.

facing page A young guest views Tara Donovan (American, b. 1969), *Untitled (Mylar)* (detail), 2010, Mylar, hot glue, H: 13 ft. Commissioned by the Indianapolis Museum of Art, Frank Curtis Springer & Irving Moxley Springer Purchase Fund, Anonymous IV Art Fund, Deaccessioned Contemporary Art Fund, 2010.218A-D.

oldfields

NEWFIELDS IS SPECIAL IN LARGE PART BECAUSE IT RESIDES on a great estate called Oldfields. With a museum, gardens, and park, Newfields is most unusual. Only a few institutions combine art, architecture, and nature in similar ways, and those—like the Huntington in San Marino, California, and the Ringling in Sarasota, Florida—can do so because they too were once great country estates.

Oldfields, former home to the families of Hugh McKennan Landon (1868–1947) and Josiah Kirby Lilly Jr. (1893–1966), is a product of the American Country Place movement of the late nineteenth and early twentieth centuries. The nationwide boom in country house building was fueled by tremendous growth in the country's economy in the years following the Civil War. The country houses and estates that sprang up outside urban areas constituted the most exclusive of suburbs, where America's wealthy gathered to enjoy their shared vision of a beautiful and restorative rural lifestyle. Both Landon and Lilly enjoyed a setting of natural beauty that enhanced the combination of architectural and landscape designs that characterized the period. While life in the country was meant to be beautiful and refreshing, it was also a place to enjoy one's family and friends—and Oldfields certainly teemed with life.

The Landons

The 52 acres that now are home to the museum and gardens were originally laid out as the rural Town of Woodstock that was developed in 1907 by Hugh Landon and a business partner. Probably responding to its location in the midst of farmlands, Landon called his estate "Oldfields" and commissioned his architect brother-in-law, Lewis Ketcham Davis, to build a grand

page 101 Installation view of the loggia during *Orchids: Cultivating Beauty*, February 10–March 5, 2017.

left Hugh Landon in his garden at Oldfields, about 1923. Historical Oldfields Photography (PHO003), IMA Archives.

above Suzette Merrill Davis Landon with daughters Margaret and Alice, 1918. Historical Oldfields Photography (PHO003), IMA Archives.

home for him and his wife. Davis designed Oldfields in a simplified French chateau style and situated it on a bluff overlooking a bend in the White River, making the most of distant views across open land to the west.

Suzette Merrill Davis and Hugh Landon and their family moved into their new 22-room mansion in 1913. Their arrival at Oldfields reflected the family's high position within Indianapolis society, culture, and business. Although born in Iowa, Hugh Landon moved as a child with his family to Kokomo, Indiana. He received a degree in 1892 from Harvard University and eventually became secretary of the Indianapolis Water Company, where his father-in-law served as vice president.

Life at Oldfields during its early days included a variety of delightful activities. The Landon daughters, for example, enjoyed parties, cutting and arranging flowers, playing with pets, walking along and fishing in the old Central Canal behind the house, and roaming the "old fields" that surrounded them. Grand gala affairs were held outside on the expansive green lawns and more intimate parties within the elegantly appointed home. However, this idyllic life was marred in late 1918 by the unexpected death of Suzette Landon at age 51.

Following his wife's death, Hugh married Jessie Spalding Walker in 1920. Later that year, they vacationed on the Maine coast, where she was enchanted by the naturalistic landscape she saw at a friend's home in North Haven. She learned that Percival Gallagher, an associate of the famous landscape firm of Olmsted Brothers of Brookline, Massachusetts, had designed the gardens. As described in the next chapter, Gallagher was soon at work at Oldfields. However, Jessie Landon died at age 60 in 1930, and although Hugh's eldest daughter and her husband came to live at Oldfields, Landon eventually sold the estate to Josiah Kirby Lilly Jr. in late 1932.

left Aerial view of the Allée and the front of Lilly House.

The Lillys

In the early 1930s, with the nation in the grip of the Great Depression, the age of large country estates was well into its twilight. However, thanks to the success of Eli Lilly and Company, the new owners of Oldfields thrived and invested in the property for more than three decades. When J.K. Lilly Jr. acquired the estate he was a vice president in the family's pharmaceutical firm, a member of the third generation of his family to provide leadership for the business. The company's founder, Colonel Eli Lilly, was born in Maryland in 1838 and moved with his family from Kentucky to Indiana in 1852. After serving as an apprentice pharmacist and in the Civil War, he established Eli Lilly and Co. in Indianapolis in 1876. From modest beginnings in a two-story building in Indianapolis, the company grew to become one of the world's most important pharmaceutical concerns.

left J.K. Lilly Jr. in his library, about 1935. Historical Oldfields Photography (PHO003), IMA Archives.

right Ruth Brinkmeyer Lilly with her children, Ruth and Joe, 1918. Historical Oldfields Photography (PHO003), IMA Archives.

above View down the Allée of the front of Lilly House, 2015.

facing page, top Vintage automobiles in front of Lilly House as a part of the program Flappers and the Flaming Youth, May 2011.

facing page, bottom Guests walking in the Oldfields gardens, 2016.

Like his father and his brother, Eli, J.K. Lilly Jr. served the family firm with a combination of specialized training, leadership skills, and business acumen. Born in 1893, he attended schools in both Indianapolis and the East before taking a degree in pharmacy from the University of Michigan. In 1914 J.K. Jr. began his career at Eli Lilly and Co. and married Miss Ruth Brinkmeyer. The couple soon had two children, Ruth and Josiah Kirby III. J.K. Jr. steadily rose through the ranks in the family business during the 1910s and '20s, proving himself an astute businessman of great vision.

Privately, J.K. Lilly Jr. was an avid collector, gathering together large holdings of historic weapons, toy soldiers, books, stamps, and coins. The last three of these collections were so large and fine that, by the time of his death, they were of international importance. Lilly's rare book and manuscript collection, for example, contained over 37,000 items and focused on notable American authors, such as Longfellow, Hawthorne, Irving, Poe, and Melville, as well as great Hoosier writers like James Whitcomb Riley and Booth Tarkington. In addition he acquired books in other subject areas, including British, European, Russian, and ancient literature; children's literature; and scientific and medical works. In 1954 he donated his book collection to Indiana University, where it forms the core of the Lilly Library. When announced in 1956, the *New York Times* called it "one of the largest and most valuable gifts of its kind ever made to an American university."

Many country house owners were, as J.K. Jr., collectors, but the country lifestyle of the time offered other recreational and gentleman-farmer interests that required significant acreage to pursue. By the standards of some country states, Oldfields was quite small—about 26-acres when Lilly purchased it—but his vision of country life extended well beyond Oldfields' boundaries. In 1934, shortly after moving to the estate, Lilly began purchasing land north of Indianapolis on which he established a model farm. At Oldfields he began to purchase the homes of the other residents in the Town of Woodstock, demolishing the buildings and adding the property to Oldfields. On this "new" land the Lillys built a house called Newfield in 1939 for their son J.K. Lilly III and his new wife, Jean Heller. The next year they constructed a recreation building just north of Newfield. The building featured indoor and outdoor swimming pools, as well as a garden to its west with a four-seasons theme. By the mid-1960s the estate covered almost all of the property of what had been the Town of Woodstock.

facing page Aerial view of Lilly House and the Rapp Family Ravine Garden with the Central Canal in the foreground, 2015.

top View of the library, 2016

above A guest reads a descriptive panel in the great hall, 2016.

overleaf, left View of the stair hall, 2016.

overleaf, right View of the great hall, 2016.

Ruth Brinkmeyer Lilly died at Oldfields in December 1965 and J.K. Jr. the following May. In 1966 their children, Ruth Lilly and J.K. Lilly III, gave the estate to the Art Association of Indianapolis, which precipitated its move from its old location on 16th Street as well as a change of name to the Indianapolis Museum of Art. Soon the museum was busy constructing a new building on the site. While the rooms in the main house at Oldfields were initially used as decorative art galleries, by the early 1990s the stately mansion and landscape were in need of attention and a fresh approach. In 1994 the museum embarked on a multi-year strategic planning process in hopes of integrating Oldfields and the adjacent property it owned in a way that would make the institution unique among American museums. The outcomes of this process were impressive. Oldfields was restored as an American country estate and the 100-acre property west of the canal was developed into an art and nature park featuring a festival area for large community gatherings. Rapid growth in the endowment during this period and the significant, annual support of Ruth Lilly enabled the institution to move forward with its ambitious goals.

In the early 2000s the home was extensively restored. Analysis allowed for the re-creation of the original paint colors and the replacement of long-vanished wall coverings. Eight hundred objects that were original to the house were identified, and appropriate substitutes were acquired for furnishings that were missing. When completed and reopened to the public in 2002, the National Register of Historic Places added Oldfields to its roster of significant American landmarks. Two years later, the estate was awarded the even more prestigious designation of National Historic Landmark, putting it in the company of the Biltmore Estate in Asheville, North Carolina, and the Hearst Castle in San Simeon, California.

Today the Oldfields residence, now called Lilly House, features eight furnished historic rooms on the main level. The majority of these rooms reflect the 1930s period of the Lilly family's occupancy, and almost 90 percent of the furnishings and decorative arts objects featured belonged to the Lillys and were used in the home. A visit to Lilly House offers a deeper understanding of life on a country estate in the early 20th century. Art and horticultural exhibitions are also held periodically on the second floor, and Christmas decorations on the estate have become a beloved family tradition enjoyed by thousands of visitors. Newfields is most grateful to the Lilly family, including Renie and Bill McCutchen, Ginny and Pete Nicholas, and Ted and Debbie Lilly, for generous, ongoing support of the Oldfields estate.

facing page, left Capodimonte porcelain figures, about 1900, on a mantel inside Lilly House, 2016.

facing page, right Orchids on display in the drawing room, 2016.

above Installation view of *Tiffany, Gorham, and the Height of American Silver, 1840–1930*, April 1–October 23, 2016, on Floor 2 of Lilly House.

overleaf, left Installation view in front of Lilly House of Karl Unnasch (American, b. 1970), *Playtime in Indy*, 2015, plastic toys. Commission. This project is part of the IMA's ARTx Series, made possible by a gift from The Efroymson Family Fund.

overleaf, right A young guest flies a kite on the front lawn of Lilly House, 2014.

the gardens

WHEN HUGH LANDON CREATED OLDFIELDS AS HIS COUNTRY estate, he chose a location that would offer tranquility and a sense of retreat, yet still be convenient to the city. More than a century has passed since then, and Indianapolis has grown up around Oldfields on every side. Yet, it still remains an oasis where sweeping lawns, tree-shaded paths, and bursts of color enchant guests.

The man who gave the estate grounds its primary character was Percival Gallagher (1874–1934). Born in South Boston, Massachusetts, he studied horticulture at Harvard where he met Frederick Law Olmsted Jr. while attending classes. In 1894 Gallagher went to work for the Olmsted firm. The venerable Frederick Law Olmsted Sr., founder of the firm and today regarded as the father of American landscape architecture, retired the following year. Except for two years (1904–1906) when he had his own firm, Gallagher spent his entire professional life in association with the Olmsted organization, where he specialized in designing residential landscapes, parks, and cemeteries. Among his assignments were renovations to the grounds of the United States Capitol and numerous estates along the Philadelphia Main Line and on Long Island. It was the estate of Thomas Lamont in North Haven, Maine, that inspired Hugh and Jessie Landon to hire Gallagher.

What Gallagher found upon his arrival at Oldfields was by no means a blank canvas, but one that nevertheless left him considerable space for the exercise of his talent. Notes from his initial visit reveal that he saw much unrealized potential as well as some unmet needs. Not surprisingly, some of his first comments were in response to the property's dominant features and characteristics: the site, the house, and the way it related to the most significant views. For example, the large terrace at the rear of the house offered expansive views from the bluff looking west across

The Allée and Border Gardens

Gallagher's Allée is the main axis of the property and provides a formal frame for the mansion's symmetrical facade. Modeled on earlier European examples, it features a great sweep of lawn lined with 58 red oak trees and stretches 775 feet from the front of the house to a large circular pool and fountain. A marble sculpture of *The Three Graces* backed by dark evergreens provides the terminus of the view. Along the length of the Allée, Gallagher designed less-formal gardens in which walking paths meander among and around irregularly shaped planting beds. Guests are drawn into these Border Gardens by the glimpse of a statue or the disappearance of a walkway around a bend. Huge, mature trees form a leafy canopy overhead, while sun and shadows play across the living corridors of foliage and flowers. At their greatest distance from the house, each Border Garden opens into the great circle of grass and water at the end of the Allée. Drawn to the fountain pool, the visitor enters the landscape's grandest and most formal space and experiences a dramatically composed view of the house, framed by the Allée's stately rows of oaks. As if floating on a sea of verdant turf, the mansion's roofline is sharply silhouetted against the blue sky.

river-bottom farmlands to similar bluffs in the distance. However, the mansion's main, east facade offered no compelling counterpoint. The "Allée," as Gallagher called it, was designed to correct this imbalance between wild and formal, while the estate's system of drives needed to screen undesirable aspects, such as Michigan Road and the nearby interurban rail line, and make the house look appropriately scaled within the landscape.

A major problem was that the estate's entrance road was fairly short, not allowing for long views of the house from afar. To compensate, Gallagher delineated the property's boundary and enhanced the sense of arrival with a high red-brick wall along Michigan Road that featured a grand pair of gates reminiscent of those at a seventeenth-century French palace. Once inside the gates, the visitor crossed over a bridge spanning the sunken interurban line. Beyond the bridge, an orchard came into view on the left and a greenhouse and cutting garden on the right—features that clearly indicated that Oldfields was an estate of substance. The road then straightened, giving visitors their first clear view of the mansion and Allée.

page 117 Water sprays from the fountain at the end of the Allée on the
Oldfields Estate, 2015. Artwork: Bertel Thorvaldsen (Dutch, 1770–1844),
The *Three Graces,* stone, 120 × 54 × 34 in. (with base). Gift of the Children of
J.K. Lilly, Jr., LH2001.227.

facing page, left Oldfields Estate Michigan Road entrance gate, about 1933.
Historical Oldfields Photography (PHO003), IMA Archives.

facing page, right Morning light in the Border Garden, 2009. Artwork: *Autumn
(Two Children with Grapes)* (detail), stone, 66 × 24 × 24 in. (with pedestal).
Gift of the Children of J.K. Lilly, Jr., LH2001.228.

above View down the Allée of the front of Lilly House, 2009.

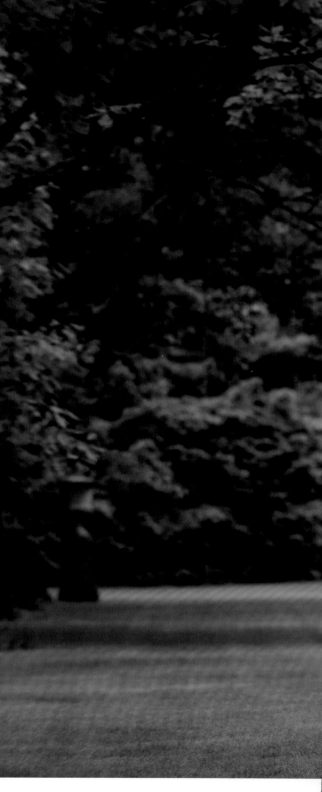

above A hummingbird moth flies by phlox flowers blooming in the Border Garden, 2016.

right Guests walk along the Allée in front of Lilly House during Family Day events, 2015.

The Richard D. Wood Formal Garden

Part of Gallagher's work at Oldfields included refreshing the Formal Garden, which was likely conceived of by architect Lewis Ketcham Davis when he designed the main house around 1911. Formal gardens incorporating strong architectural features, sculptural elements, and strict geometry were common features of country estates, and the one at Newfields is a fine example. Here a gravel pathway connects the house to the Formal Garden, descending in a pleasing rhythm of three short flights of steps before crossing a ravine by way of a limestone bridge and ascending corresponding steps to approach the garden. Flanking the entrance is a pair of white marble herms. Trellised wooden arbors supporting climbing roses mark the entrances to the garden, one at the center of each of three sides, while a fourth on the west provides shade for a garden seat. At the garden's center is a circular pool featuring a beautiful bronze fountain from which water cascades. A symmetrical pattern of gravel paths and beds filled with spring bulbs and summer annuals complete the garden. In 1993 the garden was restored through a gift from the friends and colleagues of Richard D. Wood to honor him upon his retirement from Eli Lilly and Company. Since Mr. Wood loves gardens and has served as trustee and as board chair, naming the Formal Garden for him was a fitting tribute.

facing page Summer campers work on an activity in the Formal Garden, 2013.

above Formal Garden, 2013. Artwork: *Female Herm*, marble, 84 × 24 × 24 in. Gift of the Children of J.K. Lilly, Jr., LH2001.240.

below left Fountain within the Formal Garden, 2016.

below right Fall foliage in the Formal Garden, 2015.

The Rapp Family Ravine Garden

Located between the mansion and the Formal Garden is a ravine that descends nearly 50 feet from the terrace of Oldfields to the canal below, covering more than an acre. Here Percival Gallagher designed and oversaw construction of the Ravine Garden in 1920–21 as a means of juxtaposing an informal landscape with the symmetry of the adjacent house and Formal Garden. However, by the 1990s the beauty of the Ravine Garden was a faint memory due to decades of neglect. As part of the restoration of the Oldfields estate, the Indianapolis Museum of Art undertook the revival of Gallagher's design in 1997 using the original plans, drawings, and plant lists. The $1 million project was supported by numerous organizations and individuals, and the garden was renamed in honor of the family of Dr. George F. and Peggy Rapp because of their generosity to the museum. So impressive was the result of the restoration that in 1999 the Indiana Chapter of the American Society of Landscape Architects presented the Indianapolis Museum of Art with the Centennial Medallion for re-creating one of the state's most outstanding works of landscape architecture.

The Ravine Garden is a highpoint of Percival Gallagher's work at Oldfields. In this garden one strolls on limestone-flagged paths along a rock-lined watercourse and crosses over a rustic bridge. A dense, complex planting of flowering trees, shrubs, perennials, and 19,000 bulbs creates a subtle and diffuse tapestry of color, texture, and form. The south end of the house and terrace afford splendid views into the Ravine Garden; conversely, the view of the mansion is nowhere more handsomely framed than from the Ravine Garden's paths. Adding to the pleasure of the views and the flowers and foliage is the effect of running water. At the top of the garden the trickling water's sound is hushed as opposed to the bottom where the water runs more vigorously with bubbling and splashing effects.

left The Rapp Family Ravine Garden in full bloom, 2013.

overleaf, left Koi pond in the Rapp Family Ravine Garden, 2015.

overleaf, right View from the top of the Rapp Family Ravine Garden, 2016. Artwork: Isidore Konti (American, born Austria, 1862–1938), *Nymph and Faun*, 1917, bronze, 56 × 24 × 20 in. Gift of Mr. and Mrs. John J. Weldon, 77.388.

The Madeline F. Elder Greenhouse and William and Lucy Wick Cutting Garden

Most great estates had greenhouses and cutting gardens to provide fresh vegetables, fruit, and flowers for their owners. Oldfields was no exception, and its versions were among the first things one saw after entering the gates off Michigan Road.

Originally, the estate's cutting garden was extensive and situated between the main drive and the greenhouse. During the spring, summer, and fall it would have supplied vegetables and flowers for Oldfields' kitchen and living spaces. In 2000 William and Lucy Wick made a generous donation to fund the restoration of a portion of the cutting garden. As a result, dramatic displays of dahlias delight visitors here in the late summer, while pumpkins herald the coming of fall. The remainder of the original cutting garden awaits reimagining.

• •

above View of the Oldfields greenhouses from the South, about 1933. Historical Oldfields Photography (PHO003), IMA Archives.

right The Lucy and William Wick Cutting Garden in bloom next to the Madeline F. Elder Greenhouse, 2012.

The story of Oldfields' greenhouse is more dramatic. The original structure built by the Landon family was probably replaced by the Lillys in the 1940s. By the time the organization received the property in the late 1960s, the building was in need of much repair. Preoccupied with construction of the new museum building, most of the institution's board was largely content to ignore the gardens and greenhouse for the time being, but it did create a grounds committee to advise the Indianapolis Museum of Art on landscape issues. Committee members believed their main job was to ensure that the most significant components of Oldfields' design were kept intact during the new museum's construction.

Shortly after the new museum building opened, the grounds committee became the foundation for a gardens support group, the Horticultural Society, which was established in 1972. The Society's first challenge to preserving Oldfields' history came the same year when the museum's board discussed the possibility of demolishing the greenhouse. The structure was saved, however, by an effort led by Madeline F. Elder, a long-time supporter, master gardener, and orchid aficionado. Elder and her family pledged both restoration funds and an endowment, and in association with the Horticultural Society, convinced the board to restore the glasshouse complex. Upon her death, Elder's orchid collection came to the gardens, and today viewing exotic orchids at the Elder Greenhouse is a firmly rooted tradition with garden guests. In addition to growing orchids, the greenhouse organizes seasonal displays, workshops, and periodic plant sales. The Horticultural Society has also flourished and continues to support the gardens at Newfields.

The Gene and Rosemary Tanner Orchard

The orchard was designed by Percival Gallagher during the 1920s and was, like the greenhouse and cutting garden, one of the first things visitors saw upon entering Oldfields' gates. In contrast to a commercial orchard, Gallagher meant this example to be both bountiful and beautiful. Alas, the orchard had fallen into decay by the 2000s. Its restoration in 2009 and on-going care was made possible by generous gifts from Gene and Rosemary Tanner.

....

left Orchids in the Madeline F. Elder Greenhouse, 2015.

facing page A guest viewing the blooms in the exhibition *Orchids: Cultivating Beauty*, February 10–March 5, 2017, in the Madeline F. Elder Greenhouse.

Guided by old photographs, an arched entry arbor was reinstalled and old 'Gold Rush' and 'Enterprise' apple trees were acquired from an apple farm and carefully transported to the gardens and replanted. Now standing in a long double row, the trees bloom profusely in the spring and produce green apples in the fall. Gallagher's original plan for flowerbeds beneath the fruit trees has been reimagined with peonies, irises, and Japanese anemone that bloom in succession through the spring, summer, and fall.

Opposite the apples is a large vegetable garden where heirloom varieties grow. Each year schoolchildren use the garden to learn how food is produced and land cared for by engaging with the vegetables, apple trees, and staff. Their efforts help Newfields donate produce to local food banks every year.

Newfields' horticulture staff has also broadened the orchard's purpose by promoting the role of pollinating insects, which are vital to all fruit and vegetable production. To this end, two honeybee hives and an orchard bee population are maintained. By allowing bees, flies, moths, and butterflies a place to complete their life cycle, they in turn pollinate the garden's fruits and vegetables.

The Richard A. and Helen J. Dickinson Four Seasons Garden

This lovely garden celebrates winter, spring, summer, and fall. It was designed by landscape architect Anne Bruce Haldeman of Louisville, Kentucky, for the Lilly family in 1939 to adorn the site of their new recreation building. The circular-shaped garden features a round pool with shooting jets of water at its center and four figural sculptures along its perimeter, each representing a season. A sundial tracks the hours and a grand, Neoclassical marble bench provides a place for visitors to refresh while taking in the sound of water and the sights and scents of the garden's colorful flower displays. In 2011 the Four Seasons Garden was restored through the generosity of Richard and Helen Dickinson.

facing page Summer campers walking through the gardens, 2015.

top left A young student learning about gardening and food production in the orchard, 2015.

top right Apples that will soon be picked in the orchard, 2015.

bottom Vegetables growing in the orchard, 2016.

left Allium flowers blooming in the Four Seasons Garden with Garden Terrace in the background, 2016.

below The Four Seasons Garden, 2016.

The Rain Garden

While Newfields cherishes its landscape history, not all of its gardens are original to Oldfields. In 2009 the institution furthered its desire to be as ecologically friendly as possible by creating a garden along the south side of the former interurban rail line that bisects the estate property. Rain gardens are designed to improve water quality by mimicking the natural cleansing processes of forests and meadows where rainfall is evaporated, taken up by plants, or drained into the soil within 24 to 48 hours.

The Rain Garden occupies a shallow depression that captures storm water runoff from the area near the Madeline F. Elder Greenhouse. The garden holds this water so the plants and soil are able to filter it, rather than have it rush unpurified down to the canal below, a source for Indianapolis's drinking water. The plants in the Rain Garden were chosen for their adaptability to varying soil moisture levels, made possible by vast root systems that channel water deep into the soil. Also, these plants do not require extensive use of fertilizers and pesticides, nor do they require irrigation except in periods of extreme drought. The focus on plants with contrasting scale, color, form, and texture makes the Rain Garden as beautiful as it is useful to the environment though replenished groundwater supplies, flood and erosion prevention, and wildlife habitat preservation.

The Garden for Everyone

As its name suggests, the Garden for Everyone was created to be enjoyed by all people, regardless of physical limitations. In 1988, Irving Moxley Springer gave the lead gift for the garden. Her son Michael, who had suffered from neurological disorders and had died three years earlier, was the inspiration for the generous gift. Frank Springer, Irving's husband and garden patron and Horticultural Society member, later donated an additional sum after the passing of his wife. Others contributed as well, and this special garden opened in 1993.

Claire Bennett, a landscape architect and member of the Horticultural Society, designed the garden with paved paths and raised beds that are completely wheelchair accessible. The planters feature annuals and perennials that offer visitors a multisensory experience of exciting textures and smells, as well as visual beauty from February to November. At the garden's center is a fountain featuring a bronze sculpture called *Sister of the Vault Man* by Spanish artist Pablo Serrano, which was a gift from the Joseph Cantor Collection. An inscription from Antoine de Saint-Exupéry's famous novel *The Little Prince* runs atop the garden wall surrounding the south end of the garden and reads: "It is only with the heart that one can see rightly; what is essential is invisible to the eye."

facing page, left Rain Garden, 2015.

facing page, right Coleus growing in the Garden for Everyone, 2016.

above Garden for Everyone, 2016. Artwork: Pablo Serrano (Spanish, 1910–1985), *La Hermana del Hombre Boveda*, 1963–1964, bronze, 38 × 34 × 40 in. Gift from the Joseph Cantor Collection, 1987.96.

right Rain Garden, 2015.

The Overlook Garden

Newfields' Horticultural Society's Overlook Garden was designed to blend seamlessly into neighboring existing woodland, providing occasional vistas to the Oldfields estate and its formal Lilly House, all while being an attractive feature from inside the Deer Zink Special Events Pavilion. A richly varied collection of understory small trees and shrubs such as redbud, Japanese maple, viburnum, and Carolina allspice provide interest from spring through fall, in addition to offering shelter and food for wildlife.

Beneath the woody plants is a handsome mix of herbaceous perennials and spring-flowering bulbs. Planted in large overlapping swaths at differing depths from the walk, these provide both contrasting and complementary textures and colors for both visitors and staff alike as one walks from the Overlook Garden east to the Garden for Everyone.

• •

left Sunrise during *Spring Blooms: Celebration of Color,* March 31–May 31, 2017.

below Triumph tulips in bloom as part of *Spring Blooms: Celebration of Color,* March 31–May 31, 2017.

above Tulips blooming around the Sutphin Fountain during *Spring Blooms: Celebration of Color,* March 31–May 31, 2017.

facing page Summer campers parade down the Dudley and Mary Louise Sutphin Mall, 2015. Artwork: Roy Lichtenstein (American, 1923–1997), *Five Brushstrokes* (detail), designed 1983–1984, fabricated 2012, painted aluminum, dimensions vary. Robert L. and Marjorie J. Mann Fund, Partial Gift of the Roy Lichtenstein Foundation, 2013.443A-E.4.

The Sutphin Fountain and Mall

The gardens' tram, "The Late Miss Kate," was recently funded by Charles and Peggy Sutphin in memory of Charles's late sister, Katharine. But the Sutphin family's generosity goes back generations. In 1972, for example, the iconic Sutphin Fountain was unveiled in front of the main museum building as a memorial to Samuel Brady Sutphin, a well-respected businessman whose family company pioneered many innovations in paper making. Funded by Agatha, Samuel Reid, and Dudley Sutphin, the fountain was designed by Sasaki Dawson DeMay Associates of Watertown, Massachusetts. Its main jet of water rises many feet into the air and is the centerpiece of a garden featuring 11 magnificent dawn redwoods underplanted with annuals and perennials. Around the fountain are large concrete planters filled from May to October with colorful foliage and flowering plants. Outside the adjacent Café, they are planted with evergreens and twig dogwoods in winter, while a large curved bed in front of the fountain is filled with bright annuals and tropical plants for the summer months.

Running east from the fountain for 300 feet is the Dudley and Mary Louise Sutphin Mall. Indianapolis-based architect Jonathan R. Hess designed the Sutphin Mall as part of the museum's 2004–05 expansion. The Mall is the largest green roof in Indiana, ingeniously concealing a large, underground parking garage beneath it. Another ecological benefit of the Sutphin Mall is its collection of rainwater to feed the wetlands in the Virginia B.

Fairbanks Art & Nature Park to the west of the main museum building. However, what the public sees and enjoys is the Sutphin Mall's expansive green lawns, paired rows of red maples, flower beds, and artwork.

In the middle of the Mall stands *Five Brushstrokes*, a monumental work by Roy Lichtenstein. It is considered to be one of Lichtenstein's most ambitious creations and consists of five separate elements, the tallest of which soars 40 feet into the air. The piece was the gift of the museum's Robert L. and Marjorie J. Mann Fund and the Roy Lichtenstein Foundation. The sculpture's installation on the Mall in 2014 was made possible by a gift from Ersal and Izabela Ozdemir.

Nonie's Garden

This focal point of Newfields' main entrance was created in 2008 to honor of the late Nonie (Eleanor) Krauss by her husband, John Krauss, and her friends. Nonie Krauss was very involved at the museum and loved nature, bird watching, and gardening, and thus Nonie's Garden is a fitting tribute.

Every year, major elements of the garden change with each passing season, but a group of seven sweet gum trees remain constant. These narrow upright trees, called 'Slender Silhouette,' contrast with the broad horizontal lines of the museum building. The variety was also chosen for the way the leaves change to shades of burgundy, red, orange, and yellow in autumn. To further enhance the garden's winter display, additional plants are used based on their potential to brighten the space. These may include blue weeping Alaska cedars, yews, and deciduous hollies. For a continuous show through early spring, colorful twig dogwoods and hundreds of tulips often enliven the garden. Summer displays are always lush and exuberant with color. A plaque in Nonie's Garden reads: "Here marks the passage between art and nature, nature and art, for in reality, they are one."

left View of the Dudley and Mary Louise Sutphin Mall and Indianapolis Museum of Art building in the background, 2015. Artwork: Roy Lichtenstein (American, 1923–1997), *Five Brushstrokes*, designed 1983–1984, fabricated 2012, painted aluminum, dimensions vary. Robert L. and Marjorie J. Mann Fund, Partial Gift of the Roy Lichtenstein Foundation, 2013.443A-E.4.

above Tulips blooming around the Sutphin Fountain, 2016.

overleaf View of the entrance to the Indianapolis Museum of Art at Newfields during *Spring Blooms: Celebration of Color,* March 31–May 31, 2017.

left Summer campers exploring the Virginia B. Fairbanks Art & Nature Park: 100 Acres, 2015.

facing page, top left Guests aboard the eco-friendly garden tram, "The Late Miss Kate," given in memory of Katie Sutphin, 2016.

facing page, top right Oldfields barn complex, about 1924.

facing page, bottom Summer plant combinations in the Garden for Everyone, 2015.

Food for Thought

Newfields' investment in both historic and contemporary gardens has had extraordinarily results. However, there is still much to do. The simple fact that audience research reveals that the public is four-times more likely to visit the campus if major garden and nature experiences are combined with art means enhancing the gardens and Fairbanks Park are key to the institution's future.

While a new master plan must be completed before all the details are known, Newfields is already certain that it wants to transform the abandoned bed of the Interurban Railway that transects the Oldfields Estate into an amazing garden featuring thousands of spring bulbs and flowering trees. A garden specifically designed for families where parents can engage with their children in purposeful play will also likely delight visitors in coming years.

Because scientific research has also proven that engagement with nature can improve health and brain function, and have a calming effect, Newfields also hopes to restore the Oldfields barn complex. Originally, the Arts and Crafts barn that housed dairy cows and chickens was the focal point of the estate's food-production operations. When restored and reunited with the greenhouse, flower and vegetable gardens, and the orchard, the complex could serve as a center for wellness, where visitors could learn where their food comes from and how to make healthy lifestyle choices.

virginia b. fairbanks art & nature park

THE VIRGINIA B. FAIRBANKS ART & NATURE PARK COMPRISES 100 acres of land and water that has been uniquely shaped by both natural and man-made changes in the environment. It is a landscape that reveals continuous growth and adaptation. The physical terrain of the park is notable for its variety, and includes woodlands, wetlands, a meadow, lake, river, and canal. The addition of contemporary art commissions makes Fairbanks Park one of the largest art and nature parks in the United States.

Like the evolution of this property, the development of Fairbanks Park took many years. When the Landon family built their estate on the bluff to the east, this land was a floodplain used for growing grain. Eventually, however, the Indianapolis Water Company sold the property to a local construction company, Huber, Hunt and Nichols, which excavated sand and gravel on the site to help build a portion of a nearby freeway, creating a 35-acre lake in the process. In 1972 the firm donated the acreage, lake and all, to the museum that had only recently relocated to the nearby Oldfields estate. Although the intentions at the time were to develop a park, the land lay fallow for almost 30 years before the Indianapolis Museum of Art launched its plan.

During the late 1990s a vision emerged for the park to be a "playful, adventurous, and unexpected encounter with art in nature and nature in art: always changing, always challenging." The park would "foster experiences among diverse audiences with works of art, the natural landscape, and the interaction of art and nature." In 2000, in association with Indy Parks Greenways and the Indianapolis Water Company, a site master plan was created by the California-based firm Moore Iacofano and Goltsman (MIG), and four years later an architect and landscape architect were selected to turn the vision into reality. This complicated task

page 148, center Composer Nat Evans and members of Butler University's Jordan College of Fine Arts Composers Orchestra perform *Hungry Ghosts* on the lake as part of a Fall Equinox program, 2012.

page 149 Autumnal colors on the Central Canal and Towpath that border The Virginia B. Fairbanks Art & Nature Park: 100 Acres, 2012.

facing page Guests relax in hammocks at an Autumn Equinox event, 2015.

above Guests play on and around visiondivision's *Chop Stick*, 2013.

guests to stroll, jog, and bike; to fish, walk their dogs, and watch a wide variety of animals in their native habitat; and to view great works of art. While most of the art in the park is commissioned with the understanding that it will eventually be replaced by new works, several key installations are permanent, including Jeppe Hein's amusing *Bench around the Lake*, Los Carpinteros' playful *Free Basket*, and Alfredo Jaar's reflective *Park of the Laments*.

The park is carefully managed to maximize the visitor experience, but to have as little negative impact on the natural surroundings as possible. For example, the trails that wind around the lake through the park's woods and meadows are unpaved to allow water to sink into the ground and replenish the groundwater supply. The Ruth Lilly Visitors Pavilion has a very low profile, designed to blend in with its wooded surroundings. And each installed sculptural work is created using materials that will either deteriorate naturally or have no adverse effects on the land or water. The result is a highly engaging experience that combines art and nature in imaginative, provocative ways.

However, opening the Virginia B. Fairbanks Art & Nature Park was only a beginning. Future enhancements of the park will improve visitor access by connecting the property more directly to the front of the museum and parking across the canal. Likewise, added infrastructure will make the site a place for large, public gatherings like the Penrod Arts Fair that brings more than 20,000 people to the campus each September. Simultaneously, the artistic and natural landscape will evolve through art rotations, removal of invasive plant species, growth of native trees, and the ever-changing course of the powerful White River.

Change is, in fact, the foundation upon which Fairbanks Park is built. While there are many outdoor art parks in the world, they typically focus on inserting large-scale sculptures into a cultivated landscape. Conversely, in this park the untamed landscape itself is the primary focus of the visitor's experience. To this end, the main artery of pathways is named the "Pulliam Family Landscape Journeys" to draw attention to the sense of discovery that is offered throughout the park's varied topography. The model for how the art is selected further emphasizes the importance of this natural ecosystem. Each piece is site-specific, as artists are asked to create works that take their starting points from the physical environment itself and to respond to a range of concerns about human beings' place in nature and their positive and negative effects upon it.

went to Marlon Blackwell of Marlon Blackwell Architect in Fayetteville, Arkansas, and Edward Blake of The Landscape Studio in Hattiesburg, Mississippi.

Transforming this low-lying land situated between a great bend in the White River and a nineteenth-century canal into a remarkable art and nature park was a multimillion-dollar project to which many people contributed. However, it was the Richard M. Fairbanks Foundation that made the park a reality. Fairbanks was the founder of Fairbanks Communications, which owned and operated 20 radio stations around the country. He had served on the museum's board and was very generous to the institution during his lifetime. Upon his death in 2000 the bulk of his fortune went to the Richard M. Fairbanks Foundation, which gave $4 million to develop the park in 2003 and another $11 million to the project in 2006 in honor of Virginia B. Fairbanks, Mr. Fairbanks's wife of 32 years who loved gardens and nature.

Fairbanks Park has become much loved as an urban oasis in the heart of Indianapolis since its opening in 2010. Shielded from the noise and bustle of city life by water and trees, the park enables

· ·

above Aerial view of Krannert Pavilion with the future site of the lake and park in the background. *The Indianapolis News*, November 1970, Publicity Scrapbooks, IMA Archives.

top left Jeppe Hein (Danish, b. 1974), *Bench Around the Lake* (detail), 2010, galvanized steel, yellow paint, dimensions vary. Commissioned by the Indianapolis Museum of Art, Jane Weldon Myers Acquisition Fund, Waller Fine Art Purchase Fund, Roger G. Wolcott Fund, Mrs. Pierre F. Goodrich Endowed Art Fund, Alice and Kirk McKinney Fund, 2014.103A–O.

bottom left Los Carpinteros (Cuban, founded 1991), *Free Basket* (detail), 2010, steel, paint, plastic, dimensions vary. Commissioned by the Indianapolis Museum of Art, purchased with funds provided by the Griffith Foundation Gift, in memory of Melvin Simon, 2010.217.

above Alfredo Jaar (Chilean, b. 1956), *Park of the Laments* (detail), 2010, soil, limestone, Gabion baskets, concrete, plants, wood, 144 × 2,160 × 2,160 in. Commissioned by the Indianapolis Museum of Art, Purchased with funds provided by Martha Delzell Memorial Fund, Frank Curtis Springer & Irving Moxley Springer Purchase Fund, Mr. and Mrs. Theodore P. Van Vorhees Art Fund, Jane Weldon Myers Acquisition Fund, E. Hardey Adriance Fine Arts Acquisition Fund in memory of Marguerite Hardey Adriance, The Ballard Fund, Mrs. Pierre F. Goodrich Endowed Art Fund, Roger G. Wolcott Fund, Martha M. Shertzer Art Purchase Fund in Memory of Her Nephew, Charles S. Sands, Elizabeth S. Lawton Fine Art Fund, Emma Harter Sweetser Fund, through prior gift of Wally Findlay Galleries, Chicago, Illinois in honor of William Wadsworth Findlay, Anonymous IV Art Fund, James V. Sweetser Fund, 2015.15.

Nature has long provided inspiration to artists, and the natural environment is a refuge and space for discovery, relaxation, healing, and inspiration for many people as a part of their everyday experience. Fairbanks Park provides a space for looking at art and for experiencing it in relation to the distinctive environment in which it is enmeshed. The imaginative breadth of the park sparks a sense of creativity and new possibilities in the diverse audiences who visit it, and its very special combination of both cultivated and wild landscapes allows for new possibilities of engagement with both the constructed and natural worlds.

left Cottonwood Crossing bridge, part of the pathways forming the Pulliam Family Landscape Journeys in the park, 2011.

below A heron takes flight from the lake in the park, 2012.

top left Guests enjoy a musical performance as part of Summer Solstice celebrations in the park, 2013.

bottom left Young guests playing in the park, 2012. Artwork: Jeppe Hein (Danish, b. 1974), *Bench Around the Lake* (detail), 2010, galvanized steel, yellow paint, dimensions vary. Commissioned by the Indianapolis Museum of Art, Jane Weldon Myers Acquisition Fund, Waller Fine Art Purchase Fund, Roger G. Wolcott Fund, Mrs. Pierre F. Goodrich Endowed Art Fund, Alice and Kirk McKinney Fund, 2014.103A-O.

right Aerial view of The Virginia B. Fairbanks Art & Nature Park: 100 Acres, 2015. Artwork: Atelier van Lieshout (Dutch, founded 1995), *Funky Bones*, 2010, fiberglass, plywood, dimensions vary. Commissioned by the Indianapolis Museum of Art.

miller house
and garden

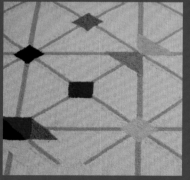

THE MILLER HOUSE AND GARDEN, OWNED AND CARED FOR by Newfields, is situated 45 minutes south of Indianapolis in Columbus, Indiana. The home and landscape were commissioned by J. Irwin and Xenia Simons Miller in 1953 and are considered one of the most important examples of Modernist architecture and landscape design in the United States. Designated a National Historic Landmark in 2000, the Miller House and Garden showcases the work of three leading twentieth-century architects and designers: Eero Saarinen, Alexander Girard, and Dan Kiley. The acquisition of the historic property and the creation of its endowment were made possible through the generosity of members of the Miller Family, Irwin-Sweeney-Miller Foundation, and Cummins Foundation. Tours of the Miller House and Garden are facilitated by the Columbus Area Visitors Center and offer visitors the opportunity to experience an integration of house and landscape that captures the genius of its designers, the aspirations of its owners, and the spirit of their time.

Joseph Irwin Miller (1909–2004) was born into a prominent Columbus, Indiana, family with business interests in banking, industry, and real estate. Miller attended Yale University, majoring in Greek and Latin and graduated Phi Beta Kappa in 1931. He received a master's degree from Oxford University in 1933 and the next year began working at Cummins Engine Company—founded by his great-uncle—that builds diesel engines in Columbus. Although beset with early difficulties, under Miller's leadership the company persevered to become the leading independent diesel manufacturer in the world.

Xenia Simons Miller (1917–2008) was born in Morgantown, Indiana, the daughter of Nellie Hosetta Wellons and Luther A. Simons. Her father was founder of the Columbus Hickory Furniture

Company and is remembered for his ingenuity and innovation in an industry characterized by traditional products and materials. Xenia Simons attended Indiana Business College before taking a position at Cummins Engine Company, working in the firm's purchasing department. Xenia and Irwin met at work and were married in 1943.

In addition to being patrons of Modernist architecture and design, the Millers were philanthropists with interests as varied as horticulture, music, historic preservation, education, and religion. They were also civic activists who were highly involved locally, statewide, and nationally. For example, Irwin Miller was the first layman to be president of the National Council of Churches and was a strong advocate for the Civil Rights Act of 1964, working with Martin Luther King Jr. to organize the March on Washington.

The Millers and Modern Architecture

Irwin Miller's grandfathers were both noted preachers in the Christian Church (Disciples of Christ), and he grew up in a multi-generational household that valued intellectual and personal engagement with religion, philosophy, politics, and music. While studying at Oxford University, holidays afforded the young scholar time for travel and exploration of continental Europe's architecture and gardens. Later in the 1930s after Miller had returned to Columbus, the local First Christian Church embarked on a major building project and turned for a design to one of Finland's leading architects, Eliel Saarinen. Though Saarinen at first declined, Irwin Miller persuaded him to accept the commission. Work on the church brought the architect's son, Eero Saarinen, also a Yale graduate, to Columbus with his father. Miller and Saarinen established a friendship that would shape the former's interest in architecture and last until the latter's untimely death in 1961.

Eero Saarinen's first commission from Irwin and Xenia Miller came in 1950, when they requested a summer house in the Muskoka region of Ontario, a popular resort area that his family had enjoyed since the late nineteenth century. In the same year, Miller commissioned a new building for the Irwin Union Bank and Trust Company, successor to the firm established in 1871 by his great-grandfather. As the church had done for Eliel, the bank would bring Eero Saarinen's brand of Modernism to downtown Columbus. Its exterior walls of glass and flat roof enlivened by a grid of nine domes shattered the image of a bank as a massive, temple-form structure, replacing it with elegant transparency.

page 158, top Alexander Hayden Girard (American, 1907–1993), *rug* (detail), 1963, wool, 274 × 146 in. Gift of Margaret, Catherine, Elizabeth and Will Miller, MH2010.21.

page 158, bottom Dining room (detail), 1953–57. The Balthazar Korab Archive, Library of Congress Prints and Photographs Division, Washington, D.C., LC-DIG-krb-00381.

page 159 Kitchen, 2013.

facing page, top West terrace and living room, 1957.

facing page, bottom J. Irwin Miller and his wife Xenia Simons Miller pose for a Polaroid in the living room with conversation pit and painting by Bonnard in the background.

right Ludwig Mies van der Rohe (German, 1886–1969), Barcelona Pavilion, 1928–29.

Collaborating with Saarinen on the bank project was landscape architect Dan Kiley.

While the bank was underway, the Millers asked Eero Saarinen to design a new residence for the family. By this time the couple had four children (a fifth would be born while the house was under construction), placing complex functional demands on the design. This house would not be a sparkling Modernist glass box, a floating, ethereal presence reflecting the landscape around it. Rather, the requirements of privacy, recreation, and service would cause Saarinen to inflect his interpretation of Modernism to accommodate them. The Millers purchased a 13-acre parcel on the outskirts of Columbus that Saarinen and his collaborators would transform into a design milestone.

Eero Saarinen

Eero Saarinen was born in Finland in 1910, and came to America in 1923 after his father won a substantial prize in a Chicago architectural competition. Soon Eliel was at work on designing and administering Cranbrook, an extensive educational complex emphasizing architecture and design in Bloomfield Hills, Michigan. Eero Saarinen assisted with designs for Cranbrook beginning in the 1920s and went on to study sculpture in France prior to enrolling in the Yale School of Architecture. Eero collaborated with his father on many projects, but in 1948 he won the competition for the Jefferson National Expansion Memorial with the soaring majesty of his St. Louis Gateway Arch, a design submitted independently of his father. The Arch brought Eero national attention and helped establish his reputation as an architect in his own right.

In the Miller House commission, Eero Saarinen expanded upon an architectural tradition developed by the famous German architect Ludwig Mies van der Rohe. Mies had designed one of the most famous buildings in the world, the German Pavilion at the 1929 International Exposition in Barcelona, Spain. This small building that became known as the Barcelona Pavilion had a flat roof supported by metal columns and walls made of glass and marble. The concept of space with a seamless flow between interior and exterior revolutionized modern architecture. For the Miller House, Saarinen used cruciform steel columns to support a flat roof and to establish a grid that informs the entire structure of the house and landscape beyond. Interior walls of marble, plaster, and glass echo the lines of this grid without following them exactly. Each corner of the grid is occupied by a function requiring privacy: master, family, and guest bedrooms, and a kitchen/service area. The central, open space of the floor grid contains the main living area of the house, which in turn flows into a dining area to the north, a sitting room to the south, and outward to a terrace on the west that overlooks the house's most significant view—a vista down a precisely angled embankment and across a broad, flat lawn that sweeps away to an irregular fringe of trees along the distant Flatrock River.

The interior's remarkable sense of soft, even light is the result of the skylight system that crosses the roof along the lines of the

structural grid, and which allows panels of the ceiling to appear to float unsupported by adjacent walls. A sunken conversation pit just off of the main living area allows for ample seating without the visual clutter that would result from additional groupings of chairs, sofas, and tables.

Throughout his career, Eero Saarinen worked within the austere geometry of international Modernism, but also created highly expressive and boldly sculptural buildings. In addition to the Miller House and St. Louis Gateway Arch, he designed such landmarks as the Dulles International Airport in Washington, DC, and the General Motors Technical Center in Warren, Michigan. Kevin Roche (b. 1922), Pritzker Architecture Prize-winning architect, became Saarinen's principal design associate when he joined Eero Saarinen and Associates in 1950. Roche played a significant role in the design of Miller House as well as many other Saarinen projects.

Alexander Girard

Architect and designer Alexander Girard (1907–1993) was born in New York, the son of an Italian father and an American mother. While his early education was in Florence, Italy, Girard later studied in London, graduating in 1929 with honors from The Architectural Association. He then trained at the Royal Institute of British Architects in London and at the Royal School of Architecture in Rome, before returning to the United States in 1932. His early associations with Eero Saarinen included his work as a collaborator on the St. Louis Gateway Arch design team. He also served as a color consultant on the General Motors Technical Center and on the Miller summer home in Canada. In 1952, Girard became design director of the textile division of the furniture manufacturing firm of Herman Miller, which had been producing the designs of Charles and Ray Eames (who also designed furniture for the Miller House) since the late 1940s.

Alexander Girard's work imbued modern interiors with strong colors and playful patterns that brought warmth and comfort to rooms that might otherwise have seemed severe and uninviting. For the Miller House, Girard designed a wide range of interior architectural details, including a 50-foot-long main storage wall and the iconic conversation pit, as well as a seasonally changing program of textiles that enlivened the interiors. Working closely with Xenia Miller, he selected ornaments and antiques to personalize the house. He also designed several rugs for the house, including one

facing page Irwin and Xenia Miller House, view from the northwest, 1957.

top Allée, view to the south. Artwork: Henry Moore (British, 1898–1986), *Draped Reclining Woman*, 1957–58.

above Allée, view to the north, 2010.

above Master bedroom sitting area with fireplace wall to the left, 2013.

facing page Living room with conversation pit in the background, 2013.

left East terrace, view to the north, 2012.

above Alexander Hayden Girard (American, 1907–1993), *gate* (detail), 1963, metal, 69 × 49 × 3 in. Gift of Margaret, Catherine, Elizabeth and Will Miller, MH2010.440.

facing page View along west terrace, 2013.

composed of emblems that represent history and associations of the Miller family. There are "Y"s for Yale, for example, and representations for each child, along with numerous other symbols of meaning to the family. Some of the chair cushions designed by Girard also feature the initials of family members. His passion for folk art is also visible in the objects chosen for the interior of the house.

Dan Kiley

Daniel Urban Kiley (1912–2004), a leading figure in modern American landscape architecture, was born in the Roxbury Highlands section of Boston. In 1932, Kiley began an apprenticeship with Warren Manning, an important figure in the field, and in 1936 entered Harvard University's landscape architecture program where he developed an interest in European Modernism and its applications to landscape architecture. He left Harvard in 1938 without completing a degree.

From 1943 to 1945, Kiley served with Eero Saarinen in the Office of Strategic Services (OSS) and following World War II received the assignment to design the courtroom for the Nuremberg war trials. While in Europe, Kiley had opportunities to experience historic landscapes and gardens, and was particularly influenced by the grand, formal tradition of designers such as Frenchman André Le Nôtre. Like Le Nôtre's influential work in the seventeenth-century gardens and park at the palace of Versailles outside Paris, Kiley's landscapes are highly structured, geometric compositions that use natural elements to create enclosed outdoor spaces.

While the interiors of Miller House afforded Girard an opportunity to enrich and personalize the house for the Millers, the garden was for Dan Kiley a canvas on which to expand Saarinen's architectural vision to the landscape. Kiley's garden—like the house itself—relies on a clear and strong geometric order, but without conventional symmetry, or paths of circulation that constrain the viewer's experience. It is largely concerned with using monocultures of trees and hedges to shape verdant views flowing from the house and spaces that function as exterior rooms.

The Miller Garden features spectacular examples of saucer magnolias and European weeping beeches, as well as beautiful arborvitae hedges, apple orchards, and a drive lined with buckeye trees. However, the landscape's grandest feature is the allée. A double row of honey locust trees define an axis along the west side of the house, extending almost to the limits of the property. With finely textured buff-colored crushed stone beneath the entire allée, the dark honey locusts stand out in sharp contrast, their lacy foliage gently filtering the sunlight.

Today Dan Kiley is considered the most important American Modernist landscape architect. Among his more notable projects are the Ford Foundation's headquarters and Lincoln Center in Manhattan; and I. M. Pei's East Building, inside and out, for the National Gallery of Art in Washington. However, many feel his garden from the Miller House to be his masterpiece and best preserved project. Kiley received the Arnold W. Brunner Prize in Architecture in 1995 and the National Medal of Arts two years later. In 2000 the Miller House and Garden became the first National Historic Landmark to receive its designation while still occupied by its original owners and while one of its original designers, Dan Kiley, was still living.

chapter eight

enriching lives

Leading through Exceptional Experiences with Art and Nature

Newfields' mission is "to enrich lives through exceptional experiences with art and nature," and the institution is uniquely qualified to fulfill this mission through its galleries, gardens, park, and historic homes. However, none of these wonderful assets would flourish and impact visitors as they do without the thousands of staff, volunteers, and patrons who have supported the institution. Thanks to their vision, hard work, and financial support the organization provides its community and region with extraordinary educational, outreach, and programmatic opportunities.

Education and Research

At its core Newfields is an educational and experiential institution. It strives to teach visitors about art and nature through a wide array of activities, ranging from building libraries, to performing scholarly research, to creating engaging activities that delight the child in all of us. While professional staff lead these initiatives, volunteers contribute greatly to the institution's success through their dedicated efforts.

Reflective of Newfields' commitment to education are the highly trained curators on staff. Through the decades the institution has been home for scores of curators whose specialties range from Asian, African, and European art to textiles, design and decorative art, and works on paper. All the while, curators of contemporary art scan the horizon looking for the best artists of our own age. Through their great work the museum has produced thousands of exhibitions, publications, and public programs that have advanced the knowledge of art and educated the public.

above Guests enjoying the Avant Brunch curated experience in the Caroline Marmon Fesler Gallery, 2014. Artwork: Julianne Swartz (American, b. 1967), *Terrain* (detail), 2008, 14- and 18-gauge colored electrical wire, speakers, and sound, 240 × 692 × 347 in. (installed). Martha Delzell Memorial Fund, 2010.69.

facing page, top A young guest interacts with an iPad app in the exhibition *The Essential Robert Indiana*, February 16–May 4, 2014, in the Allen Whitehill Clowes Special Exhibition Gallery. Artwork: Robert Indiana (American, b. 1928), *1968 Black and White Love*, 1971, ink on paper, screenprint, 30 × 30 in. Museum Purchase through Multiples, Inc., 71.88.9A.

facing page, bottom A guest participates in a bonsai class at the Madeline F. Elder Greenhouse, 2016.

page 169 A guest listening to the audio guide while viewing the exhibition *Matisse, Life in Color: Masterworks from The Baltimore Museum of Art,* October 13, 2013–January 12, 2014, in the Allen Whitehill Clowes Special Exhibition Gallery. Artwork: Henri Matisse (French, 1869–1954), *The Yellow Dress* (detail), 1929–1931, oil on canvas, 39⁹⁄₁₆ × 32⅛ in. The Baltimore Museum of Art: The Cone Collection, formed by Dr. Claribel Cone and Miss Etta Cone of Baltimore, Maryland, BMA 1950.256

Over the years many of these projects have received national and international acclaim.

Since moving to the Oldfields estate in 1970, the staff has included a wide range of horticulturalists who have deep training in botany, garden history and landscape design, plant selection and propagation, and forestry and greenhouse management. Together these talented individuals create, oversee, and interpret Newfields' unique array of natural resources, including the gardens of the Oldfields estate, the Virginia B. Fairbanks Art & Nature Park, and Miller House and Garden, which have received a variety of state and national awards.

To support its educational activities, a library was founded in 1909. Today the Stout Reference Library, Horticultural Society Library, and Archives are open to the public, staff, docents, and scholars to facilitate serious research or simply to provide a place to relax while reading about art or nature. In total the two libraries contain over 100,000 volumes, including books, magazines and journals, auction catalogs, ephemera files, and museum, garden, and art dealer publications from around the world. Both of the libraries have taken generations to build and would not have developed into such important resources without the generous backing of long-time supporters and trustees like Eleanor Evans and Erwin Cory Stout and the Horticultural Society.

The Archives collects, preserves, and makes accessible the historical records produced by the museum, gardens, and estates, as well as documents and photographs that are related to the history of the institution. Formally established in 2010, the Archives contains over 1,000 linear feet of museum records, manuscripts, personal papers, ephemera, scrapbooks, photographs, videotapes, films, and artifacts that chronicle the history of the institution since its founding in 1883. In addition, the collection includes papers from individuals, such as trustees, directors, and staff; records of its Board of Governors and affiliated organizations; and other primary research materials related to its historic properties.

These library and archival collections support a wide range of research performed by curators, horticulturalists, conservators, and scientists that enable the institution to produce scholarly books and articles, as well as an astounding array of public programs like exhibitions, symposia, and lectures. To share such works as widely as possible, the institution has become a leader in digital publishing and videography, exploring various publication and distribution

science laboratory thanks to a $2.6 million grant from the Lilly Endowment, a $1.75 million matching grant from the Andrew W. Mellon Foundation, and a $1.5 million bequest from Otto N. "Nick" Frenzel III, a longtime Indianapolis philanthropist and former museum trustee. Through the addition of this analytical laboratory, Newfields supports research and publication by museum curators, conservators, scientists, and horticulturalists and continues to build its reputation as an industry leader in the fields of art conservation and collections care.

In today's society data is growing at an exponential rate. The institution's information science professionals seek to turn this endless stream of data into useful information and knowledge for the public as it relates to art, nature, and science. To accomplish this goal, IMA Lab was founded in 2009. Today the Lab is a multi-disciplinary, award-winning web design and development consultancy that serves Newfields as well as other cultural institutions throughout the country. Its team represents a wide range of technical expertise and backgrounds, including digital strategy, information architecture, branding, web design and development, custom software development, mobile and iPhone applications,

models within this emerging field, including platform selection, accessibility, design, and enhanced multimedia content.

To ensure the care of its art collection and to support the work of its curators, in 1952 the museum became a charter member of the Intermuseum Conservation Association and founded its own Conservation Laboratory in 1970. Since then the institution's efforts have expanded to include highly skilled staff trained in the conservation of paintings, works on paper, textiles, and three-dimensional objects. Research and treatments performed by conservators inform the understanding of artwork in the museum's collection and establish protocols for its ongoing care. Also, the staff actively contributes to the international conservation community through the publication of these efforts and the development of collaborative projects with external institutions and researchers. In 2013 the museum's conservation program received the coveted Ross Merrill Award for Outstanding Commitment to the Preservation and Care of Collections, presented annually by Heritage Preservation and the American Institute for Conservation of Historic and Artistic Works.

Allied to art conservation is conservation science, which is concerned with the material and chemical aspects of artwork, its interaction with the environment, degradation mechanisms, and the immediate and long-term effects of conservation treatments. In 2011 the museum opened a state-of-the-art conservation

and deployment/systems integration. The Lab is dedicated to the creation of open-source software and aims to benefit the entire cultural technology community by exploring innovative ideas, designing applications, building useful products, and sharing them with others.

Education and Community Impact

Newfields serves a wide and varied public. For more than a century the institution's ability to engage local, regional, and national audiences through stimulating programs and activities has steadily grown. A major advance took place following World War II, when the museum saw a resurgence of attendance by the general public and schoolchildren. This increase resulted in greater demand for gallery tours, so three women were recruited to serve as volunteer guides in the spring of 1946. Soon, others completed their training, and the museum's well-respected docent program was born. In 1992 the horticulture staff and volunteers began giving tours, effectively launching the Garden Guides program. Today there are nearly 200 individuals who dedicate many volunteer hours in training and leading the public through Newfields' galleries, gardens, park, and historic homes.

Research has proven that children who are exposed to cultural experiences at a young age typically continue attending institutions like art museums and gardens throughout their lives. Therefore, the education of children and families is particularly important to Newfields, and staff and volunteers dedicate much of their resources to reaching this segment of the community. One such group is the Alliance of the Indianapolis Museum of Art that was founded in 1958. From the start, the Alliance has been interested in education for its members and for the public. To that end, it has supported book publishing, exhibitions, and lectures, along with art acquisitions. One of its most recent initiatives was the creation of the IMA Alliance Family Education Fund that supports important educational programs for families and children at the museum and in the wider community. Fine examples of Newfields' efforts to engage younger audiences include the country's first preschool in a general art museum, created in 2015 in partnership with St. Mary's Child Center; the Toddler Art Group; the After School Program; the Viewfinders outreach program to elementary schools in Indianapolis, Washington and Pike Townships; Summer Camp; the Teen Council; and the Teachers Education program. Through

page 172 A young guest shows off paint-covered hands at the IMA Block Party, 2014.

page 173 Summer camp participants pose in front of the installation in the Efroymson Family Entrance Pavilion, 2014. Artwork: Sopheap Pich (Cambodian, b. 1971), *A Room* (detail), 2014, bamboo, resin, aluminum, metal, 36 × 26 (diam.) feet. Commissioned by the Indianapolis Museum of Art.

facing page, top A conservation fellow performs a restoration treatment, 2016. Artwork: Neroccio di Bartolommeo de' Landi (Italian, 1447–1500), *Madonna and Child with St. John the Baptist and St. Mary Magdalene* (detail), about 1495, tempera on wood, 28 × 20⅛ in. Indianapolis Museum of Art, The Clowes Collection, 2004.161.

facing page, bottom A guest views plants available at the annual Perennial Premiere event, 2013.

above A young guest participates in an event at Spring Equinox: Celebration of Flight, 2012.

these efforts the lives of thousands of children and families are enhanced each year.

Engaging with visitors of all ages and abilities is also central to Newfields' mission, and it therefore offers an extremely wide range of programs targeted at specific groups, including the elderly and those with special needs. For example, it has created a program led by specialized docents for Alzheimer patients. Developed in partnership with the Alzheimer's Association and designed for individuals with early-stage Alzheimer's, this program provides an opportunity for participants to engage in conversations about art and nature with their care partner, family, and friends. Docents also hold a regular public tour each month for deaf and hard-of-hearing visitors that is accompanied by an ASL interpreter. For visitors who are blind or visually impaired, the museum offers regular tours incorporating a combination of touch and audio description.

Beyond targeted programs like the preschool and tours for Alzheimer patients are events that welcome very large and highly diverse audiences. The most popular of these is the Penrod Arts

Fair that has happed at Newfields each September since 1967. Now one of the premier art and craft fairs in the country, the Festival has become an Indianapolis tradition and annually welcomes over 20,000 patrons to Newfields' campus where it showcases hundreds of artists and offers live music, performing arts, and local cuisine. Proceeds from this one-day celebration provide grants for Indianapolis-area arts and community organizations, including the museum.

facing page Chris Kallmyer performs for guests in the galleries as part of the Fate Conference, 2015. Artwork: Frederick Wilson (American, 1858–1932), designer, Tiffany Studios (American, est. 1837), manufacturer, *Angel of the Resurrection* (detail), 1903–1904, stained glass, lead, 348 × 168 × 4 in. Gift of the First Meridian Heights Presbyterian Church, Indianapolis, 72.75.

left Summer Campers view Alyson Shotz (American, b. 1975), *Wave Equation* (detail), 2010, stainless steel, silvered glass beads, aluminum, 120 × 144 × 117 in. (installed). Anonymous IV Art Fund, 2013.262.

right A young guest becomes a pirate during a Summer Camp, 2014.

page 178, left Guests taking part in Martin Luther King, Jr. Day celebrations, 2013.

pages 178–9, right Guests enjoying Summer Solstice celebrations in the park, 2014.

facing page Guests viewing a collection object in closer detail, 2016. Artwork: Theodor Groll (German, 1857–1913), *Washington Street, Indianapolis at Dusk* (detail), 1892–1895, oil on canvas, 76 × 98½ in. Gift of a Couple of Old Hoosiers, 72.133.

left Guests gather for The National Bank of Indianapolis Summer Nights Film Series in the Amphitheater, 2013.

Across this wide spectrum of activity, Newfields constantly seeks to improve its offerings to the public and has therefore developed a robust audience research and evaluation department. Through the efforts of its talented staff and volunteers the institution carries out the following types of audience research and evaluation: studies on visitor motivation and how people engage with different interpretation approaches to works of art and nature, online visitor segmentation, exhibition and program evaluation, evaluation of interpretive materials, and usability testing. To gather information from its visitors, Newfields utilizes comment cards, surveys, timing and tracking studies, qualitative interviews, focus groups, visitor profile and experience surveys, non-visitor research, and prototype and design testing. Much of this research is done in association with outside collaborators in an effort to advance knowledge within the museum and garden fields. However, the primary goal is to learn from its visitors, so Newfields can constantly improve its offerings and remain relevant as society changes through time.

Through the decades the institution's education and engagement efforts have continued to grow, and today its Division of Public Programs and Audience Engagement is nationally recognized. Within this division are the departments of Academic Programs and Learning Research; the Docent Program; Interpretation, Media, and Evaluation; and the Libraries and Archives. Overall, the talented staff in these areas create and manage more than 100 highly diverse and innovative programs annually. These activities are geared toward visitors with varying experience levels and cultural perspectives; are often produced in partnership with other institutions in the city; and are held in a wide variety of locations within the museum building, gardens, park, and historic homes. One of the museum's longest-running programs is the venerable Summer Nights Film Series, which has been held for more than 40 years, with The National Bank of Indianapolis as the series title partner since 2012. Other program highlights include Martin Luther King, Jr. Community Day, Solstice and Equinox events, art history and horticultural classes, and "behind-the-scenes" tours.

visions of the future

chapter nine

Growing from a Strong Foundation

Since its founding in 1883 the Indianapolis Museum of Art at Newfields has grown into the largest visual arts organization in Indiana and is now a beloved and important cultural cornerstone of the community and region. This accomplishment has happened because of many people and their passions. Without the support of its volunteers, patrons, and staff, the museum would not have flourished.

During the course of its development, the organization fortunately has had thousands of donors who generously gave of their possessions, time, and funds to build in Indianapolis a cultural center where art and nature can be experienced in amazing ways. In 2016 alone, for example, there were more than 300 works of art acquired by the museum and nearly 40,000 volunteer hours contributed by individuals, including the many hours dedicated by members of the Board of Governors. From individuals, corporations, and foundations, approximately $17.6 million in gifts were made, while thousands of people attended events that occurred on Newfields' campus. Although the number can really never be known, millions of visitors from around the globe have experienced the wonders of this place for nature and the arts.

While transformative donations of artworks, property, and funds from individuals and foundations are recorded elsewhere in this volume, broad support from within the overall community has been vital to advancing Newfields. The Lilly Endowment has been the institution's greatest financial supporter, having over a long period of time made grants totaling more than $45 million. Many private individuals have come together to form donor societies because of their passion for the museum, gardens, park, and historic homes. To celebrate the organization's centennial in 1983,

Newfields a place of excellence for nature and the arts. It is a place where people of all ages and backgrounds engage with 5,000 years of great art from civilizations around the world, have life-changing educational experiences on a host of relevant topics, and enjoy the beauty and healing power of nature in the form of a verdant estate garden and urban park. Vision, passion, and generosity have made all this possible, enriching countless lives for the better.

Becoming a Living Museum of the Future: The Plan, 2015—2025

The economic recession of 2008–09 was a bellwether event. Suddenly the institution's endowment lost over $100 million of its value and reductions in staff and programs had to be made. Significantly, more than the standard 5% was drawn from the endowment to cover operating expenses, and principal payments were not made on the outstanding $122 million in bond debt that was generated by the expansion of the museum and gardens in the mid-2000s. By 2013 the institution was in weak financial condition, which propelled the board and staff to develop a new plan for moving forward.

for example, the Second Century Society was formed by donors who wanted to make a significant annual gift. The Society endures today and has approximately 200 members who collectively donate over $1 million annually to Newfields. Similarly, the Founders Society celebrates those whose lifetime giving has surpassed $100,000, while the Legacy Society is composed of individuals who have remembered the institution in their estate plans. Periodic capital campaigns have also been successful because of great acts of generosity and passion for the organization's mission. The campaign in the mid-2000s to expand the main building and to make it more accessible resulted in several multi-million dollar gifts, including those from Randolph H. Deer and Wayne P. Zink, the Efroymson Family Fund, the Richard M. Fairbanks Foundation, and an anonymous donor. In 2006 Melvin and Bren Simon pledged $10 million to endow the directorship, and more recently the Lilly Endowment granted another $10 million to establish an endowed Innovation Fund that will enable Newfields to identify, research, and pilot new programs and campus improvements anticipated to substantially increase earned and contributed revenue. Such investments, along with those that came before, have made

1935 BUGATTI TYPE 57 COMPÉTITION

page 182, center A young guests plays on Atelier van Lieshout (Dutch, founded 1995), *Funky Bones* (detail), 2010, fiberglass, plywood, dimensions vary. Commissioned by the Indianapolis Museum of Art.

page 182, bottom Pierre Auguste Renoir (French, 1841–1919), *Bouquet in a Vase* (detail), 1878, oil on canvas, 18¾ × 13 in. The Lockton Collection, 70.80.

page 183 Installation in progress of the exhibition *Graphite,* December 7, 2012–June 2, 2013, in the June M. McCormack Forefront Galleries. Artwork: Judith Braun, *Without Pleasure All We'd Have Is a Bunch of Stuff Vibrating* (detail), 2012, powdered graphite on vinyl, dimensions vary. Courtesy of the artist. Commissioned by the Indianapolis Museum of Art.

facing page, left Toddler Art Group participants walk around the fountain at the end of the Allée in front of Lilly House, 2013.

facing page, right A guest walks through the exhibition *Dream Cars: Innovative Design, Visionary Ideas,* May 3–August 23, 2015, in the Allen Whitehill Clowes Special Exhibition Gallery. Vehicle: *Bugatti Type 57 Compétition Coupé Aerolithe* recreation, 1935. Designed by Jean Bugatti and Joseph Walter; made by The Guild of Automotive Restorers. Courtesy of Christopher Ohrstrom.

above Guests gather for The National Bank of Indianapolis Summer Nights Film Series in the Amphitheater, 2014.

In May 2015 the Board of Governors unanimously approved a new strategic plan designed to guide the institution to 2025, and the next year extended the contract for Dr. Charles L. Venable, the current Melvin & Bren Simon Director and CEO, so he will remain at Newfields until 2026. This vision strongly embraces the fact that the institution is unique in the United States in the way it can combine art and nature to enhance the lives of its visitors and the health of its community. Beyond galleries full of great art, Newfields has three historic homes, a variety of gardens, and an urban park and natural ecosystem—all spread over three sites.

Supported by such extraordinary assets Newfields can fulfill its mission "to enrich lives through exceptional experiences with art and nature" in ways few other institutions in the world can. By more fully realizing the potential of its art, historic architecture, gardens, and parkland, the board and staff strive to increase attendance, increase financial support, and increase Newfields' impact on visitors and the community. The accomplishment of these goals will build a stronger place for nature and the arts in a variety of ways. Quality of life in the region will improve as more individuals and families visit Newfields to participate in programs they feel are relevant to their lives. Success will attract and retain exceptionally talented staff and volunteers whose creativity will energize the institution. Additional earned income and philanthropic support will be generated as more visitors decide to become members and foundations and private donors come to understand Newfields' enhanced commitment to engaging a wider and more diverse audience. Together these forces will ensure that Newfields is both a financially sound and programmatically vibrant cornerstone of art, nature, and innovation for generations to come.

Underpinning Newfields' ability to have greater community impact and to significantly improve its financial foundation is the vision of becoming a major destination for a wider audience. Innovation and investment are vital to achieving this goal. As recognized recently by the Lilly Endowment when it gave a major grant to perpetually fund innovation at Newfields, art museums must reinvent themselves if they are to remain broadly relevant and reach their full potential to positively impact their communities. Researchers have shown that new audiences prefer experiences that are active, immersive, and social, rather than those that focus on observation and quiet reflection. This relevance gap between classic, core programming models and what contemporary

above Guests take part in activities at Family Day: Marionette Menagerie, made possible by a gift from Bob and Toni Bader, in the Pulliam Family Great Hall, 2016.

facing page My Botany summer camp tour of the Madeline F. Elder Greenhouse, 2016.

audiences—particularly young people—increasingly value in cultural experiences has resulted in declining attendance and membership figures at many cultural institutions nationwide. For example, museum attendance over the last two decades has remained relatively flat despite the significant expansion in facilities between 2005 and 2010. Furthermore, its core audience of repeat visitors has traditionally come from a relatively narrow demographic range.

The change in Newfields' admission policy instituted in early 2015 is an important example of the kind of institutional change that is fundamental to the success of the new strategic plan. Unfortunately, providing free admission did not drive attendance as hoped; in fact, nearly half of the potential new visitors surveyed were unaware of the free admission policy. The reintroduction of a general admission charge and the designation of a single entrance to the museum and gardens greatly enhanced the perceived value of the Newfields experience to the public. First-time guests now

say they appreciate the value of entry to the museum, special exhibitions, and gardens for one all-inclusive fee, and are staying significantly longer when they visit. Membership, currently counted at over 17,000 households, is at its highest level in the history of the institution, supplying Newfields with a broader audience of repeat visitors and increasing both contributed and earned income.

New programming has also enhanced the guest experience at Newfields. Over the past several years with the full support of the Board of Governors, staff has invigorated traditional programs like exhibitions through the introduction of technology-based learning tools and by carefully listening to guests about what they want from their experience. Innovative programs for individuals and families that bring local visual and performing artists together with visitors in the galleries, gardens, and park now abound. Newfields' film series and performing arts events have been rethought to make them more appealing to a younger and broader audience thanks to innovative staff and major funding from the Efroymson Family Fund, a CICF fund. Even 3- to 5-year-olds now learn in the first art- and nature-based preschool in an American encyclopedic art museum.

Imagining the Future Together

The future of Newfields, with its museum, park, and gardens, is both vibrant and challenging. Despite the huge expansion in

left Installation view of Spencer Finch (American, b. 1962), *Following Nature* (detail), 2013, glass, coated glass, polyester filters, metal, glass panel: 23⅛ × 23¼ × ¼ in. (each). Contemporary Art Society Fund, Anonymous IV Art Fund, 2013.263.

right Theodore Clement Steele (American, 1847–1926), *Street in Vernon*, 1886, oil on canvas, 18 × 28 in. Gift of Jack and Marjorie Lee Farr Family, 2016.2.

facilities in the 2000s, the institution's full-time staff has been steadily reduced to approximately 200 employees, which is the same size it was in the early 1990s. Similarly, the annual operating budget has declined to approximately $21 million, which is equal to that of 2001 when adjusted for inflation. Facility maintenance is an eternal challenge, and today it is estimated that $43 million is required to correct outstanding issues with buildings and properties in the coming decade. Plus, there is the institution's bond debt that must be paid off over the next 20 years. Significantly, the first debt repayments began in 2014, and approximately $100 million remains outstanding.

However, the vitality, generosity, and creativity of its supporters and staff will no doubt enable Newfields to both maintain its status as having an art museum of excellence and secure a more sustainable financial future. While using no more than a 5% draw from the endowment, Newfields wants to become a central thought leader in Indianapolis where critical ideas of our time are explored. Newfields must become an institution so vital to our community that no one can imagine a future without it.

As Newfields moves to make art and nature equal partners in how it serves the community, those who love the museum because of traditional art will not be disappointed, and neither will those who appreciate avant-garde, contemporary art. The Indianapolis Museum of Art at Newfields will continue to acquire realist works like T.C. Steele's *Street in Vernon* from 1886, which was recently given by the Jack and Marjorie Lee Farr Family, and it will also push boundaries with acquisitions like Spencer Finch's *Following Nature*, which perfectly unites art and nature through its luminous reflections inspired by light playing on Claude Monet's lily pond in Giverny, France.

However, to be an innovative place for nature and the arts, the institution needs to more fully embrace its great natural resources as never before. Research has proven that engagement with nature improves overall health and brain function. Furthermore, audience analysis shows that identifying the campus as an art AND nature destination increases the likelihood to visit fourfold beyond the attraction of a stand-alone art museum. Hence, we have given the name "Newfields" to the campus as a whole, while maintaining the well-known title of "Indianapolis Museum of Art" for the museum.

Art and nature are clearly a powerful combination. In thinking about how they can come together at Newfields in the years to come director Charles Venable said in his 2016 Annual Meeting address:

We want the public to think of us as a truly vital force in our community . . . as a place that inspires lifelong learning and wellness . . . as we now do through the preschool . . . and will in the future do through a farm-to-table food program.

We want the public to think of the IMA as a place that celebrates diversity . . . as we now do through our international art and plant collections . . . and will do by forging a broader array of community partnerships going forward.

We want the public to think us as a place that nurtures creativity and innovation . . . as we now do through innovative programing that engages visitors as never before. Thanks to a $10 million grant in 2015 from the Lilly Endowment, we are now the only museum in America, if not the world, to have an endowed innovation fund to ensure institutional vitality for years to come.

Finally, we want everyone to think of us as a place that sustains life on our fragile planet . . . as we now do through the reconstruction of native habitats for plants and animals in Fairbanks Park . . . and will do by more actively teaching our visitors about how they can personally make a difference.

If through art and nature Newfields can successfully inspire lifelong learning and wellness, celebrate diversity, nurture creativity and innovation, and help sustain life on a fragile planet, the future citizens of Indiana can be assured that Newfields will still be an amazing place for nature and the arts when it celebrates its 200th birthday in 2083—a place of wonder that the present generation sustains and champions for future generations.

top left Guitarists prepare for Stuart Hyatt's sound installation *E is for Equinox* in The Virginia B. Fairbanks Art & Nature Park: 100 Acres as part of the 2014 Autumn Equinox Community Day supported by The Hagerman Group. Artwork: Type A (American, founded 1998), *Team Building (Align)* (detail), 2010, aluminum, steel cables, telephone poles, 2 rings of 30 in. circumference, each. Commissioned by the Indianapolis Museum of Art.

center left A guest views Jacco Olivier (Dutch, b. 1972), *Revolution* (still), 2010. HD animation. Duration: 24 min. Courtesy of the artist and Marianne Boesky Gallery, New York.

bottom left A volunteer assists with the planting of a labyrinth composed of native Indiana grasses in the park, 2016.

facing page Sunset on the Dudley and Mary Louise Sutphin Mall, 2014. Artwork: Roy Lichtenstein (American, 1923–1997), *Five Brushstrokes*, designed 1983–1984, fabricated 2012, painted aluminum, dimensions vary. Indianapolis Museum of Art, Robert L. and Marjorie J. Mann Fund, Partial Gift of the Roy Lichtenstein Foundation, 2013.443A-E.4.

Generous support for this publication was provided by Kay Koch as well as The National Bank of Indianapolis

THE NATIONAL
BANK of INDIANAPOLIS

With original contributions by Dr. Charles L. Venable and text adapted from IMA publications *Every Way Possible: 125 Years of the Indianapolis Museum of Art*, *The Story of the IMA*, *Miller House and Garden*, and *Oldfields*.

Published by the Indianapolis Museum of Art
4000 Michigan Road
Indianapolis, Indiana 46208-3326
www.DiscoverNewfields.org

ISBN: 978-0-936260-82-2

Editor Dylan Remeš Jensen
Produced by Lucia | Marquand, Seattle
Designed and typeset by Susan E. Kelly
Typeset in Ideal Sans and GT Eesti Display
Assistant Director of Photography Tascha Horowitz
Manger of Rights and Reproductions Anne M. Young
Senior Photographer Eric Lubrick
Color Management iocolor, Seattle
Printed by C&C Offset Printing Co., Ltd., Shanghai, China

Front Cover Sunrise on the Dudley and Mary Louise Sutphin Mall, 2014. Artwork: Roy Lichtenstein (American, 1923–1997), *Five Brushstrokes*, designed 1983–1984, fabricated 2012, painted aluminum, dimensions vary. Robert L. and Marjorie J. Mann Fund, Partial Gift of the Roy Lichtenstein Foundation, 2013.443A-E.4 © Roy Lichtenstein Foundation. Photo by Eric Lubrick.

Back Cover Frank Weston Benson (American, 1862–1951), *Sunlight* (detail), 1909, oil on canvas, 32 × 20 in. John Herron Fund, 11.1 © The Frank W. Benson Trust.

p. 175: Support for St. Mary's Child Center at the Indianapolis Museum of Art is provided by The Indianapolis Foundation, a CICF affiliate, and The Alliance of the IMA. Toddler Art Group is supported by a grant from the PNC Foundation. The IMA's Teen Arts Council is supported by Bob and Toni Bader and a grant from The Indianapolis Foundation, a CICF affiliate. IMA After School is made possible through generous support from The Alliance of the IMA. Viewfinders is supported by a grant from the Junior League of Indianapolis.